THE FILMS OF

MEL GIBSON

Other books by John McCarty

Nonfiction
The Complete Films of John Huston (Citadel Press)
Movie Psychos and Madmen: Film Psychopaths From Jekyll and Hyde to Hannibal Lecter (Citadel Press)
Thrillers! Seven Decades of Classic Film Suspense (Citadel Press)
The Modern Horror Film (Citadel Press)
Hollywood Gangland: The Movies' Love Affair With the Mob
The Little Shop of Horrors Book (with Mark Thomas McGee)
Alfred Hitchcock Presents (with Brian Kelleher)
Splatter Movies: Breaking the Last Taboo of the Screen
You're on Open Line: Inside the Wacky World of Late Night Talk Radio (with Bill Miller)
The Amazing Herschell Gordon Lewis (with Daniel Krogh)

Fiction
Deadly Resurrection

Anthologies
The Sleaze Merchants: Adventures in Exploitation Filmmaking
The Fearmakers: The Screen's Directorial Masters of Suspense and Terror
John McCarty's Official Splatter Movie Guide Vol. 1
John McCarty's Official Splatter Movie Guide Vol. 2

THE FILMS OF
MEL GIBSON

REVISED AND UPDATED

John McCarty

CITADEL PRESS
Kensington Publishing Corp.
www.kensingtonbooks.com

CITADEL PRESS books are published by

Kensington Publishing Corp.
850 Third Avenue
New York, NY 10022

All Kensington titles, imprints, and distributed lines are
available at special quantity discounts for bulk purchases
for sales promotions, premiums, fund raising, educational,
or institutional use. Special book excerpts or customized
printings can also be created to fit specific needs. For
details, write or phone the office of the Kensington special
sales manager: Kensington Publishing Corp., 850 Third
Avenue, New York, NY 10022, attn: Special Sales
Department, phone 1-800-221-2647.

Citadel Press and the Citadel logo are trademarks of
Kensington Publishing Corp.

Designed by Andrew B. Gardner

First printing: September 2001

10 9 8 7 6 5 4 3 2 1

Printed in the United States of America

Library of Congress Control Number: 2001091819

ISBN 0-8065-2226-7

Photo Credits and Copyrights:

ABC Television Network
American-International Pictures
Andrew Cooper
Associated R&R Films Pty Ltd.
Avalon Films
Buena Vista Distribution, Inc.
Carolco
Central Motion Pictures Corporation
Murray Close
Columbia Pictures Industries, Inc.
Dino De Laurentiis Corporation
DreamWorks Pictures
Garthrope Inc.
Melinda Sue Gordon
Icon Productions
Icon Distribution Inc.
Intertropic Films
Ladd Company
Joseph Lederer
Lorey Sebastian
Mad Max Pty Ltd.
MGM/UA Entertainment Co.
NBC Television Network
Orion Pictures Corporation
Paramount Pictures Corporation
Pisces Productions Pty Ltd.
Time Warner
Touchstone Pictures
Stanley Tretick
Tri-Star Pictures, Inc.
Universal City Studios, Inc.
Viacom
Walt Disney Pictures
Joel Warren
Warner Bros., Inc.
World Icon NV and Icon, Inc.

Contents

Preface

I must confess that when I agreed to undertake *The Films of Mel Gibson* for Citadel Press, I was not a Mel Gibson fan.

This is not to say I disliked his work as an actor (I wouldn't have agreed to do the book if that had been the case); merely that I had never given it much thought. Most of his films I had not seen, and those I had seen I'd been drawn to not by the fact that Gibson starred in them but by their subject matter, genre, or the talents behind the camera—my primary interests as a writer about films.

Like everyone else who loves movies, I have my favorite stars, but whereas they may be the most visible members of a movie's collaborative team and account for its box-office success, they do not actually *make* the movie—unless, of course, they write and/or direct it as well. Therefore, they've never held much interest for me as a possible subject for the kind of film book I prefer to write.

Contrarily, the idea of turning my hand to examining the career of a major star did have a certain change-of-pace appeal. Not only would it be an opportunity to *try* something new, but if I was lucky enough to find the right subject, I might *learn* something new as well—the process of discovery being as important for a writer as it is to the reader.

Thus, when *The Films of Mel Gibson* was proposed to me by Citadel, I considered it carefully. Mel Gibson was a major star, all right; they don't get much bigger. But because he'd also worked with some of the best filmmakers in the business (like Peter Weir) and was beginning to

initiate his own projects, and even direct them, I knew there would be material for me to fall back on if the subject of Mel the Actor turned out to have little or no meat. So I said yes and, as it happens, was very lucky indeed. Researching and writing *The Films of Mel Gibson* (which included screening *all* his movies and seeing those I'd already seen again) proved to be an eye-opening and rewarding experience.

I did learn something new—a lot, in fact—not only about Mel Gibson the actor but about the astonishing superficiality of much of the so-called film criticism in this country. Reviewers (note many examples in each chapter) have been so blinded by, or prejudiced against, Gibson's matinee-idol looks that they have seldom given his acting talent (even after playing Hamlet) or passionate commitment to filmmaking the serious consideration both have long deserved.

Putting it simply, there's more to this guy than the star quality that meets the eye; more remarkably, that "more" is not a recent development signaled by his winning an Oscar. It's been there all along.

In his acerbic memoir *Adventures in the Screen Trade*, veteran screenwriter William Goldman counseled aspiring scriptwriters to ignore the following basic Hollywood rule at their peril: "Stars will not play weak and they will not play blemished," he wrote, "and you better know that now."

If this is the rule (and with most stars it is), the writers of Mel Gibson's films—veterans (such as Goldman himself) and novices (such as *Braveheart*'s Randall Wallace) alike—have failed to learn or take heed of it, and with good reason: Gibson ignores it, too. In fact, he's spent most of his career playing characters with weaknesses and blemishes, a predilection going back to even his earliest screen roles.

Like Clint Eastwood, whose career Gibson's somewhat resembles, though their acting styles are diametrically opposite (minimalist Clint versus maximalist Mel), Gibson has consistently pushed the envelope of his star power and appeal by doing what Eastwood biographer Richard Schickel calls "stretching the audience's support" in his choice of roles. This inclination seems to have been a governing principle of both actors long before they became stars with enough audience support to even try stretching.

For example, each played remorseless killers (Clint's "Man With No Name" in Sergio Leone's no-budget spaghetti western *A Fistful of Dollars;* Mel's Mad Max in George Miller's no-budget homage to Leone's movies) against all odds that such antiheroic screen behavior would endear them to an audience, much less pave a path toward stardom. Much later, Clint had his rogue cop *Dirty Harry* and Mel his suicidal cop Martin Riggs in *Lethal Weapon.* Subsequently, both men turned to directing. The parallels go on and on.

Moreover, specific themes pop up with remarkable consistency in the films of Mel Gibson—both films in which he had no hand in initiating as well as pet projects. This indicates that his choice of projects and roles wasn't willy-nilly, even early on, when he didn't have enough clout to be selective and his projects chose him. Among these themes: the pain of growing up, coming to grips with responsibility and reaching maturity—a troublesome, and troublemaking, process that extends even into adulthood, as Gibson the man as well as the actor knows well. The theme is present in Mel Gibson's very first film, *Summer City,* hardly a "personal project." There are many more, as this book will show, demonstrating that even an actor can be a film's auteur as much as the writer and director.

A final word about this book. While a certain amount of biographical information is included in it, it is not a biography. Gibson has turned down offers to pen his own autobiography or submit to an "authorized" one (ridiculous enterprises both for all but commercial reasons, since he's a young man with many years and many movies ahead of him) and has elected not to participate in any of the numerous "unauthorized" books on his life published since he became a superstar. He believes that even a movie star is entitled to some privacy, works hard to maintain it for himself and his family, and feels that whatever his fans need to know or are entitled to know about him which is of importance is right up there on the screen for them to see. So gossip hunters should look elsewhere.

The Films of Mel Gibson confines itself to Gibson's work on the screen and in the director's chair. Nevertheless, as many of his films are not only self-referential but self-revelatory, a distinct portrait of the man emerges from that work. And on that note, let's go looking.

Acknowledgments

My appreciation to the following for their research efforts on my behalf, for supplying me with illustrations and other materials, and for their invaluable support of this project overall:

Eric Caidin, Cheryl McCarty, East Greenbush Library, Rob Edelman, Hollywood Book and Poster, Film Favorites, Jerry Ohlinger Movie Materials, Inc., Audrey E. Kupferberg, Michael Lewis, Putnam Valley Historical Society, Linda Rauh, Stephen Sally, Steve Schragis, Ardis Sillick, Michael McCormick, Westchester Historical Society Library, and Andrew H. Zack.

INTRODUCTION

"Mad Mel"—An Actor, Not a Star

Mel Gibson's 1995 Oscars in the Best Picture and Best Director categories for his epic *Braveheart* signaled a new direction for this international superstar once superficially hailed by *People Weekly* as "the Sexiest Man Alive."

No longer content to be one of the few actors whose name on the marquee almost guarantees a film's success, the now-forty-plus-year-old American-born but Australian-reared actor has committed himself to spending as much time behind the camera as in front of it—to call *all* his own shots. And he has sufficient prestige and clout in the film industry to get his way, having entered the select group of actors whose international popularity nets him a whopping $20-million-plus salary per picture.

Not bad for an actor who first came to prominence in an Australian-made cult movie, *Mad Max,* in which his distinctive voice was dubbed by the film's American distributors because his "Aussie" accent was deemed "incomprehensible" to American ears. And who may never even have been heard of in his native land of America were it not for the Vietnam War and the explosive emergence of a revitalized Australian film industry in the 1970s and 1980s.

Mel Columcille Gerard Gibson was born on January 3, 1956, in Peekskill, a small Hudson River

Once hailed as the "Sexiest Man Alive," Mel has frequently gambled with this superficial aspect of his popularity by taking on image-busting roles.

town referred to in many magazine profiles of the actor as "upstate New York."

Amusingly, New York City residents refer to it the same way, as they do any town or city in the state which is located north of Manhattan. In fact, the pre–Revolutionary War Dutch hamlet, settled in the eighteenth century, is one of the oldest towns in the state; it's about a half hour's drive out of Manhattan, hardly "upstate" if you live, as I do, in the "outback" of the state's capital region.

The sixth of eleven children (five girls and six boys), Mel Gibson is of Irish-Catholic and Australian ancestry. The name Mel, as he told writer Tim Cahill in a 1988 *Premiere* magazine interview, is not short for Melvin or anything else. "It's Mel . . . actually an old Irish name. They've got a cathedral in Ireland called St. Mel's."

His middle name, Columcille, derives from the area of Ireland where his late mother, Anne, was born. It is Gaelic, meaning "dove of the church." The Gibson family is quite devoutly Catholic, Mel included. Among his least-known film credits is a 1992 religious documentary, *Greatest Stories Ever Told: David and Goliath,* which he narrated. He and his wife, Robyn, do not practice birth control and are opposed to abortion. His father, a staunch traditionalist as far as church doctrine is concerned, has published a number of controversial books over the years that were critical of some of the more liberal Vatican II doctrinal changes.

Mel Gibson's great-grandfather on his father's side emigrated from Ireland to Australia in 1862. The family's name was Mylott; it produced a daughter, Eva, who grew up to become one of Australia's most renowned opera singers in the early part of this century.

Eva Mylott moved to America shortly before World War I and not long after married a southerner named John Hutton Gibson, who had interests in the tobacco business. They had two sons, Hutton II (Mel's father) and Mylott. Although she lived in America until her death in 1920, Eva Mylott Gibson never gave up her Australian citizenship, which would have important consequences for the family years later.

Hutton Gibson II inherited his mother's gift for singing but didn't pursue it as a career. Nor did he pursue a career in business, like his father. Instead, he became a brakeman for the New York Central Railroad. An insatiable reader (which Mel Gibson is, too, though he didn't go in much for reading in his youth, preferring TV and movies instead), he used his wide knowledge on a variety of subjects to hit the $20,000 jackpot as a contestant on the TV quiz show *Jeopardy* (accomplishing this during the Art Fleming years, not the Alex Trebek ones). With the prize money, he moved his wife, and the eleven Gibson children around, eventually settling in a bigger house a bit farther "upstate," in the area of Salisbury Mills (just south of Newburgh) in 1962.

Shortly thereafter, Hutton Gibson suffered an on-the-job back injury that put him on permanent disability. Concerned about his older sons' being drafted to serve in the controversial Vietnam War and having no job to hold him down, he decided the time was right to move the family again—this time as far away as possible—and used the $475,000 disability settlement to move the entire Gibson clan to his mother's homeland.

Australia has very strict immigration laws. You get to settle there via citizenship of a family member or if you have a firm offer of employment. Hutton Gibson didn't have the latter, but he did have the former, so off the family went in 1968, the tumultuous high point of the Vietnam controversy in America, settling in Sydney.

Twelve years old at the time, at first Mel Gibson found the uprooting difficult to come to terms with. "The kids made fun of me and called me Yank," he told an interviewer in 1983,

"and I had a fairly rough time of it."

The Gibsons retained their American citizenship even after becoming permanent residents of Australia, so Mel Gibson remains a Yank to this day, and an unnaturalized Aussie, too.

Given the screen image of reckless bravado that has made Mel Gibson an international star and box-office draw, it is surprising to find that most people who knew him in his early years, friends and teachers alike, described him as "basically quite shy." Many friends and colleagues insist that despite his fame and cover-boy status, he is still shy—that his image as an extrovert is a mask.

Nevertheless, the young Gibson did have a reputation for being a bit of a hell-raiser—perhaps to offset his shyness, a characteristic of many performers—and for possessing an irreverent sense of humor. He also delighted in hearing as well as telling dirty jokes and making outrageous puns.

Always fond of slapstick in general and the Three Stooges in particular, he would sometimes do pratfalls in public and perform other feats of comic daring at unexpected times to keep his mates in stitches. His escapades led to his being nicknamed "Mad Mel."

Sensing perhaps some inherited theatrical genes, Mary, one of Gibson's older sisters, suggested he apply for admittance to the prestigious National Institute of Dramatic Art (NIDA) at the University of New South Wales after his graduation from high school in 1974. Gibson was uninterested and decided to bum around instead, doing a variety of backbreaking odd jobs that made him conclude that he wasn't much interested in that type of work, either. He thought of becoming a chef.

On the sly, his sister got an application form from the NIDA, filled it out, forged his signature, and sent it in. Called for an audition, Gibson was initially upset by what his sister had done, then thought, What the hell, and went to the interview.

"They made me do all these silly things—improvise, sing, dance . . . I was terrible," he told an interviewer in 1981. But when the audition committee asked him why he had applied and sought to become an actor, his blunt

Clean-cut cop turned black-clad avenger: Mel Gibson as Mad Max, the character that established him as an action star.

response—"I've been goofing off all my life. I thought I might as well get paid for it"—so amused them that he was accepted. "I guess they saw something raw in me," he now says.

Patterned after the Royal Academy of Dramatic Art, London's rigorous actors' training ground, the NIDA put Gibson through the paces, making him cavort onstage in virtually every type of role, from bit parts to leads to women's parts, such as Queen Tatiana in a production of Shakespeare's *Midsummer Night's Dream*. He got to play Romeo as well, opposite future Australian film star and fellow student Judy Davis's Juliet, in another Shakespearean classic more befitting of his future screen image.

While studying at the NIDA, Mel Gibson also made his film debut, in a low-budget "beach buddy" movie called *Summer City* (1976); it was cast with a number of his fellow students, including his close friend and roommate Steve Bisley, who played the lead. Mel's was a supporting role, but the billing would be reversed in his next film, *Mad Max* (1979).

Gibson says of his first screen-acting role: "My character was a nineteen-year-old surfer who simply surfed and acted dumb, which was all I could possibly handle at the time. The movie actually got a release, but fortunately only in Australia." He was paid four hundred dollars for his work in the film.

Perhaps because of this inauspicious beginning, Gibson decided that films were not for him, so after graduating from the NIDA in 1977, he aggressively pursued work in the theater and on television instead.

He joined the State Theatre Company of South Australia that same year, landing the leads in productions of *Oedipus* and *Henry VI*. After leaving the company, he appeared in many other stage productions, including *Waiting for Godot, Romeo and Juliet* (again), a long-running war drama called *No Names, No Pack Drill* (in which he played an American), and in a brief hiatus from his subsequent film career, Arthur Miller's *Death of a Salesman,* in which he played the title character's disillusioned son Biff. He also worked on a variety of Australian television shows, including a soap opera called *The Sullivans.* Acting on "the soaps," he said, was the most disagreeable experience of his professional life so far—worse, even, than the rigors of making *Summer City.* He reconsidered: Maybe film work wasn't so bad, after all.

Ironically, and with great good fortune, he came to this conclusion just as the perpetually fledgling Australian film industry was finally on the verge of coming into its own and exploding around the world as a major filmmaking force.

Filmmaking in Australia has a rich tradition extending as far back as 1906. Though nowhere near as prolific as the American, British, and other film industries at the time, Australia turned out more than 150 feature-length films during the silent period alone. The films were made wholly by Australians, for Australians, about Australian subjects, and received little or no distribution elsewhere in the world, but Australian audiences made them profitable by attending them in record numbers.

The situation began to change as the talkies arrived and other world filmmaking centers, particularly Hollywood, began to dominate everywhere. Crowded out of theater space in favor of the more lavishly produced Hollywood and British productions, which Australian audiences were as hungry to see as everyone else, domestic production slowed to a trickle.

The government attempted to counter this in the late 1920s by instituting a system that would ensure domestic product a "quota" of theater space, but the system did little to step up slowed production, and between 1930 and 1970 feature films produced in Australia by Australians numbered just a few dozen. The primary industry became newsreels, for which Australian filmmakers soon gained an international reputation—a period in the country's filmmaking history that was nostalgically recalled in director Phillip Noyce's 1978 Australian film *Newsfront.*

To seek their filmmaking fortunes, or just to get work, Australian actors, directors, writers, and technicians were compelled to go elsewhere. Some went to England, others to America, their mass exodus placing a further drain on ambitions for a revived Australian film industry.

Until Mel Gibson came along, the only international star produced by what little film industry existed in Australia was a leathery character actor named Chips Rafferty. And the film that made his name, a World War II adventure called *The Overlanders* (1946), while produced in Australia by Australians, was financed by a British company, Ealing Films.

The situation began to change again in the 1960s, at just about the time the Gibson family was planning its move to Australia, when the government called for the establishment of a national film and television school to train talent and the creation of a film commission to fund the development of Australian films, TV programs, and documentaries through a system of tax breaks and subsidies.

Eventually, two filmmaking centers arose, one of them based in Sydney, the other in Mel-

The name is Mel, an old Irish name: "They've got a cathedral in Ireland called St. Mel's."

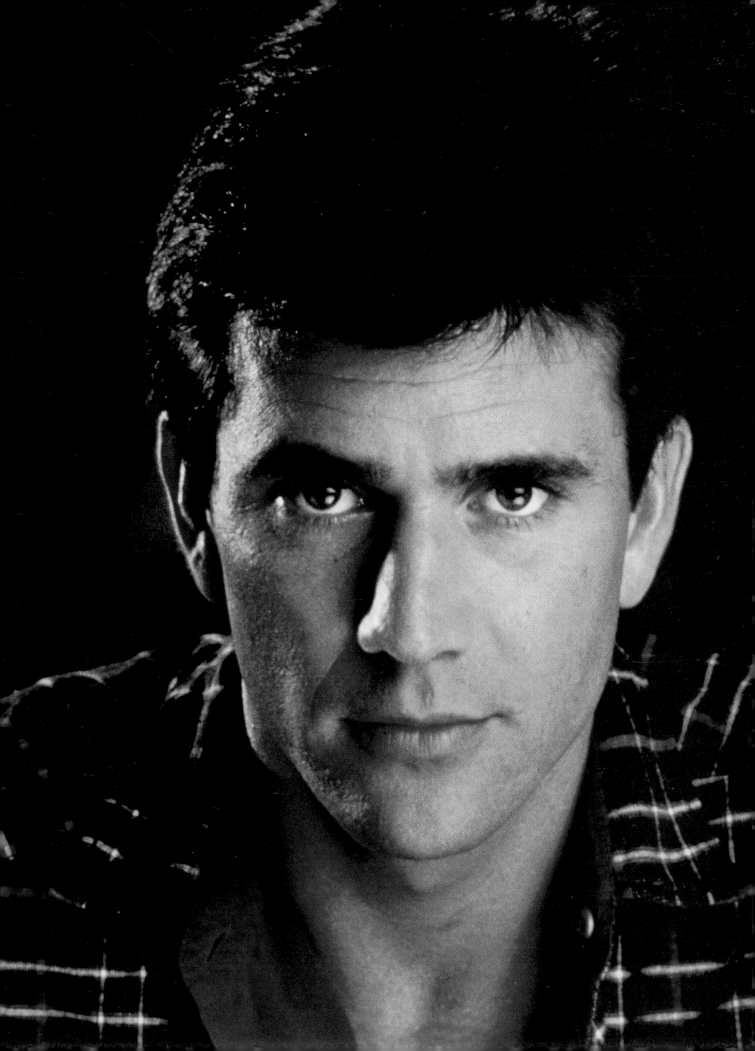

bourne, and by 1970, filmmaking in Australia began to gain a momentum it had not seen since the early 1920s. (Each Australian state now has its own film body that funds movies through tax incentives and subsidy support.)

Budgets were restrictive, however, with a million-dollar ceiling imposed on each film. "It was not an arbitrary decision," Francis O'Brien, the American executive producer of Mel Gibson's breakout hit *Gallipoli* (1981), told me. "It was soundly economic. You see, if you made a movie in Australia for more than a million dollars, you'd never get your money back because there's only fourteen million people in the country to go and see it."

In other words, the Australian film industry still considered its films for domestic consumption primarily, assuming international exposure would be hard to come by.

O'Brien said that mounting a film like *Gallipoli*, a period war film with a $3 million budget, required outside sources of funding—in that film's case, the deep pockets of two Australian tycoons, Robert Stigwood and Rupert Murdoch.

Outside sources of funding also became a requirement if a project submitted to the Australian Film Commission for development and state funding didn't meet with the commission's approval.

Such was the case with Mel Gibson's second foray into screen acting, the controversial *Mad Max*.

Mad Max, an apocalyptic action movie set in Australia "a few years from now," after the rest of the world has been ravaged by nuclear war and oil is at a premium, was written by novice filmmaker George Miller and a writer-economist named James McCausland.

Among other things, this story of a clean-cut young highway patrolman, or "interceptor" of lawbreaking bandits of the open road, who goes ballistic and becomes a high-speed avenger when his wife and child are run down by a marauding biker gang, was a satire of Australia's national obsession with the automobile. Perhaps because of the country's bigness, this obsession with wheels, or "car culture," is not dissimilar to our own in America.

Director Peter Weir's cult hit *The Cars That Ate Paris* (1975), which was retitled *The Cars That Ate People* for its American release, funded by Australian state grants in 1974, had satirized this culture, as had other Australian "road movies," which also received state funding. However, when the script of *Mad Max* was submitted to the Australian Film Commission for a state funding recommendation, it got a firm thumbs down!

Though not opposed to action movies per se, those who made recommendations for funding movies to the various state bodies under the commission umbrella viewed Miller and McCausland's script as little more than a crass exploitation picture with an eye on the dollar and "all the moral uplift of *Mein Kampf.*" Funding was denied.

Miller and his producer, Byron Kennedy, had to look elsewhere to get financing for their demolition derby, which, though not even made yet, had already stirred up as much controversy as the Marlon Brando biker movie *The Wild One* had (*Mad Max* pays more than a few homages to this classic movie) when it was released in America in 1954.

Miller, who had graduated from the University of New South Wales Medical School before turning his hand to filmmaking, used his income as a practicing doctor to help fund the picture. (He says he got the inspiration for the film from attending to so many road-accident victims in emergency wards.) Meanwhile, Kennedy sought backing from owners of car-repair shops, independent distributors, and anyone else he could hustle until the film's budget of $375,000 was finally secured.

Next came the search for the right actor to play the clean-cut cop turned black-clad avenging road warrior of the title. Miller had seen *Summer City* and called Mel Gibson in for an audition.

Shortly before the interview, Gibson got involved in a barroom brawl and showed up looking more like the burned-out, banged-up Max of the sequel (*Mad Max 2: The Road Warrior* [1981]) than the clean-cut Max of the first film.

One eye was swollen, and his face "looked like a busted grapefruit," Gibson says. He looked every inch his nickname of "Mad Mel." For Miller and Kennedy, this translated quickly

As Frank, with Mark Lee as Archy, in Peter Weir's Gallipoli. *Gibson won his second Australian Best Actor Award for his performance.*

to "Mad Max," and Gibson got the part and his first big break on the international film scene, for *Mad Max* was one of the first of the new wave of Australian movies to become a global hit, earning more than $100 million in rentals worldwide.

The film was even picked up for distribution in the lucrative American market, a tough nut to crack for any foreign film outside of the art-house circuit. To offset the stigma of its

being a foreign film, *Mad Max*'s U.S. distributor, American-International Pictures (AIP), a specialist in exploitation movies which had produced a number of biker and car action films in the past, such as Roger Corman's *Wild Angels* (1966), had the dialogue redubbed by American actors, jettisoning the "indecipherable" Australian voices (including Gibson's) for a more home grown sound.

In fact, if you listen to the sound track

The young Gibson had a reputation for being a bit of a hell-raiser.

closely, it appears that, perhaps as a cost-cutting measure, the Australian voices were redubbed only where AIP deemed it most necessary—as there are spots, usually involving patches of dialogue of one word or two, where Gibson's voice and that of Steve Bisley, who plays Max's sidekick Jim Goose, are clearly their own.

Ironically, America was one of the few countries in which *Mad Max* was not a megahit theatrically. Nor were Gibson's next two films, *Tim* (1979) and *Attack Force Z* (a.k.a. *The Z Men* [1981]), the former getting an American release via the art-house circuit only, the latter receiving exposure just on video and television.

Tim was based on an early novel by Colleen McCullough, the Australian authoress whose most recent novel, *The Thorn Birds,* had become a huge international bestseller. The film's writer and director was Michael Pate.

One of the many Australians who had sought work in America during the lean years, Pate had become an established character actor there, appearing in more than thirty films, among them the 1965 western *Major Dundee* (1965), for Sam Peckinpah, and the oddball horror-western *Curse of the Undead* (1959), in which he played a black-clad Mad Maxian gunslinger who also happens to be a vampire.

When the moribund Australian film industry began to rise from the dead, Pate returned to his native country and turned his hand from acting to writing and directing. *Tim,* the sentimental story of a lonely, middle-aged woman (Piper Laurie) who befriends a slow-witted young handyman, then falls in love with him, was intended by Pate as a starring vehicle for his son Christopher, also an actor. However, other young actors were called in to test as well—among them, Mel Gibson. Since *Mad Max* had not yet been released, Gibson was not faced with having to compete for the change-of-pace role against his soon-to-be-established screen image as an action hero. He struck Pate as an affable but shy young man and the perfect Tim. He got the part, and his performance earned him his first Best Actor Award from the Australian Film Institute, the Australian equivalent of the Oscar, in 1979.

Gibson segued from the low-key, heart-tugging *Tim* straight into another action movie, the World War II adventure *Attack Force Z,* about a squad of American and Anzac Special Forces troops sent on an impossible mission to rescue

an important diplomat whose plane has crashed on a Japanese-held island. The cast reflected the squad's multinational makeup: American John Phillip Law, New Zealander Sam Neill, Australian John Waters, and Australian-American Mel Gibson.

The assigned director was Phillip Noyce, a graduate of the Australian National Film School, who had a number of award-winning films under his belt, such as the earlier mentioned *Newsfront*. Script difficulties, combined with the producers' insistence that Noyce start shooting before those difficulties were ironed out, prompted Noyce to abandon the project. He was replaced by Tim Burstall, another prominent Australian director with a larger list of award-winning credits than Noyce.

Under the circumstances, production was

Gibson and director George Miller (right) *take a break during the filming of* Mad Max 2: The Road Warrior, *a dangerous film to make. Producer Byron Kennedy was killed in an unrelated helicopter accident shortly after the film was completed.*

The Bounty *presented a revisionist view of Fletcher Christian as a callow youth who "went native."*

The Bounty *presented a revisionist view of Fletcher Christian as a callow youth who "went native."*

a headache from start to finish, but the film *was* finished and went on to enjoy some success in Australia and a few overseas markets, not including the United States, where it finally received distribution on tape and cable TV two years after its initial release—by which time Gibson's name had become something to capitalize on.

Another obscure Australian film that would capitalize on Gibson's stardom for exposure in the years ahead was *Chain Reaction* (1980), a rip-off of the 1979 nuclear-jitters thriller made in America, *The China Syndrome* (1979). Retitled *Nuclear Run* for its videocassette release, the film starred Gibson's old chum Steve Bisley, with a "special appearance by Mel Gibson." Reports film historian Rob Edelman: "Gibson's participation is not 'special.' There's a sequence in an auto body shop. A mechanic rolls out from under a car. He is shown in close-up in one shot, lasting a second, and he's played by Mel Gibson. It's his only moment in the film." For Gibson completists, however, that may be enough.

Gibson called *Attack Force Z* a fiasco (". . . though it did my career no harm," he says) and has been quoted as attributing the films shortcomings, somewhat uncharitably, to the "hack direction" of Tim Burstall. In contrast, Burstall has said he got on quite well with Gibson and predicted after the troubled film wrapped that he'd be "amazed if Mel isn't in Hollywood in the next twelve months." Alas, it took a bit longer, but not much.

It was during this period that Gibson married Robyn Moore, a dentist's aide in Sydney. Given the amorous perks that typically come with being a good-looking screen heartthrob, and a bachelor at that, it is surprising that Gibson married so early; in fact, he and Moore had been friends for six years before graduating to a romantic relationship. He told a friend that he wanted to settle down and was just not meeting the

13

In spite of his leading-man looks, character roles are what Mel Gibson prefers.

"right kind of women"—that is, Catholic, interested in marriage, and desirous of a big family. Robyn Moore was all those things.

The two were married in 1980. They had their first child while Gibson was away in Egypt shooting location scenes for *Gallipoli*. Still very much married today, the Gibsons now have six children, two of them twin boys. (The genes for producing twins are supposed to skip a generation. But not in Gibson's case, for two of his brothers are twins also.)

In the crazy world of show business, Robyn Gibson remains, as Mel describes her, his "Rock of Gibraltar, but prettier."

Born in 1944, the son of a Sydney real-estate broker, Peter Weir, the director of *Gallipoli*, seemed destined to follow in his father's footsteps until the film bug bit him. He gained his experience hands-on, without the benefit of a film-school education. He began making experimental shorts in 16 mm, graduated to features with the cult hit *The Cars That Ate Paris*, and

burst upon the international film scene with his hypnotic essays on the occult and cultural collision, *Picnic at Hanging Rock* (1975) and *The Last Wave* (1977), as the Australian film industry began to boom.

In many ways, it is Weir who is responsible for the superstardom Mel Gibson enjoys today. For although *Mad Max* had exposed Gibson to an international audience, the two films he made almost back-to-back for Weir revealed to that wider audience something his performance in the little-seen *Tim* had already indicated— that he was capable of more than just cartoon-like action heroics. *He could act.*

In addition, the two films for Weir further helped to define Gibson's evolving screen persona—that of the reckless adventurer whose devil-may-care attitude, air of bravado, and propensity for high risk-taking borders on the irresponsible, even irrational, but whose

The future superstar, who now earns $20 million plus per film, was paid just $400 for his screen debut in Summer City.

courage eventually pushes him over the line from rascal to responsible hero.

As more than one critic has noted, Gibson's screen characters, from Mad Max to William Wallace in *Braveheart* (1995), are not so much leaders as men with strong qualities of leadership who pave the way for and enable real leaders to emerge. It is a recurring theme in Gibson's more serious work and seems to interest him a great deal.

Gallipoli is Peter Weir's patriotic hymn to the legendary 1915 military disaster that claimed the lives of thousands of young Australian fighting men in World War I. The subject had been dealt with on-screen before in Anthony Asquith's *Battle of Gallipoli* (a.k.a. *Tell England* [1931]). But Weir's was a more personal view of this tragic bloodbath that defined the Australian national character and which Australians liken in iconography to the American defeat at the Alamo.

Says Weir in the film's press book:

> I was thinking of a story set in France, dealing with the battles of 1916–1917, then someone said to me why not make the film about Gallipoli. I wrote a story outline and gave it to David [Williamson, the film's screenwriter]. Our first approach was to tell the whole story from enlistment in 1914 through to the evacuation of Gallipoli at the end of 1915, but we were not getting at what the thing was, the burning center that had made Gallipoli a legend. So we put the legend to one side and simply made up a story about two young men, really got to know them, where they came from, what happened to them along the way, spent more time getting to the battle and less time on the battlefield. *Gallipoli* is about two young men on the road to adventure, how they crossed continents and great oceans, climbed pyramids and walked through the ancient sands of Egypt and the deserts of the outback to their appointment with destiny. The end of the film is really all about that appointment and how they coped with it.

The two young men are Archy and Frank. Archy, played by newcomer Mark Lee, making his screen debut, is the more idealistic and patriotic of the duo. In contrast, Mel Gibson's Frank is a pragmatist. Lured to enlist by the siren call of adventure, his chief goal thereafter is to ensure his survival. He is a youthful version of the pragmatic heroes in *Stalag 17* (1953) and *The Bridge on the River Kwai* (1957), played by William Holden, the actor to whose screen persona Gibson's has sometimes been compared.

"I was impressed with Mel Gibson after *Mad Max*, and [producer] Pat [Lovell] was, too," Weir says of his casting choice. "So Mel was a mutual thought and not hard. He was like a diamond in the rough." This was the identical quality of Gibson's character, Frank.

Gibson won his second Best Actor Award from the Australian Film Institute for *Gallipoli*. As expected, the film was a huge hit in Australia. Unexpectedly, it was a success everywhere else, too—and a modest one even in America, where most people had never heard of Gallipoli. American producers saw in the film that Gibson had given a star-making performance, although it would take several more years and several more roles—including a reprise of his Mad Max character—in several more films before he would be catapulted to Hollywood.

Richard Donner, who would direct Gibson in more films than any other director, has described him as a character actor with a leading man's face.

Many of Gibson's fellow students at the NIDA who witnessed his performances in a variety of character roles in stage productions, such as *Waiting for Godot*, confirm this, saying that if it weren't for the good looks that have typed him as a matinee idol and leading man, he would excel in the kind of character parts played by someone like Gene Hackman, the kind of roles he prefers.

Some of Gibson's most daring acting gambles—*Hamlet, The Man Without a Face, Braveheart*—as well as his performances (the hero as semipsychotic) in such commercial ventures as the smash hit *Lethal Weapon* series, are evidence of this. As is the sequel to *Mad Max, Mad Max 2: The Road Warrior*.

Gone in *Mad Max 2* are the clean-cut-looking Max of the first film and the fresh-faced Frank Dunne of his previous film, *Gallipoli*.

Gibson and Spacek played a calamity-plagued farm couple in The River.

Dressed in a dirty black-leather outfit, his dark, close-cropped hair now sprinkled with gray, his face is cut up as the result of too many scrapes with outback outlaws, and his eyes (one of them practically scarred closed) reflect a lifetime of experience. Even though the sequel picks up young Max's story just a short time after the events of the first film, Gibson, the burgeoning screen superstar, masks himself in a seedy, gone-to-hell look that renders him almost unrecognizable.

Whether Gibson had it in mind or not, this was the kind of professional gamble Dustin Hoffman had taken after shooting to stardom as the clean-cut hero of *The Graduate* (1967) by playing a burned out, tubercular, low-life anti-hero in *his* next film, *Midnight Cowboy* (1969). And the result was much the same. No, Gibson didn't get an Oscar nomination for his performance in *Mad Max 2,* but he further demonstrated his acting range in the image-busting role. The film was an international blockbuster,

17

18

earning more than $20 million alone in the United States, where the first *Mad Max* had gone virtually unseen.

With a budget roughly ten times larger than they had on the first film, director George Miller and producer Byron Kennedy were able to give *Max 2*'s apocalyptic landscape a more futuristic, gonzo look, earning kudos from science-fiction fans everywhere. They were also able to pump up the quota of furious adrenaline-rushing action, already considerable in the first film, to ever-greater heights of daredevildom. *Mad Max 2* contains some of the most astounding action scenes and stunt work of any film made anywhere up to that time. It became the template for every high-octane, non-stop-action thriller turned out everywhere ever since.

Unfortunately, producer Byron Kennedy, a helicopter enthusiast who was involved in staging many of the film's extraordinary action set pieces, didn't live to see the film become an international blockbuster. He was killed in a helicopter accident in 1979, after the film wrapped and was in postproduction.

Gibson called *Mad Max 2: The Road Warrior* a dangerous film to make. Despite every precaution taken, many of the film's stunt people wound up in the hospital with broken bones and lacerations. Preferring to do his own stunts, or as many as the production's insurance company would allow, Gibson got bruised and banged up as well. But the dangers to life and limb involved in the making of *Mad Max 2* were only a warm-up for his next film, the aptly titled *The Year of Living Dangerously* (1983).

A love story about an Australian journalist (Gibson) and a British embassy aide (Sigourney Weaver) who fall for each other in Dakarta amid the tumultuous 1965 collapse of the corrupt Sukarno regime as the result of a Communist coup d'état—a bloodbath that claimed almost a million lives—the film was shot in the Philippines. Ironically, opposition to the corrupt Marcos regime was beginning to trigger the same kind of violent unrest there that was being portrayed in the film.

Director Peter Weir was scheduled to film a scene of a Dakarta mob stoning the U.S.

As the embattled, and resolutely stubborn, Tom Garvey in The River.

embassy in protest of Sukarno's relationship with the West. Six thousand Moslem extras were hired and made up to play Indonesian protesters for the elaborate scene staged in Manila's Muslim quarter. Then some political extremists circulated through the crowd, spreading the word that the film was anti-Muslim. Anger flamed, and the extras began shouting real death threats against the filmmakers; these continued later, by letter, then by phone. Weir and Gibson received anonymous death threats over the telephone nightly.

Weir decided that the volatile atmosphere he was attempting to capture on film was becoming dangerously real. "I wasn't prepared to take the risk that someone would die," he told the *New York Times*. He moved the production back to Australia, where it was completed.

Gibson said later: "I didn't really think we were in any real danger in Manila. We were given too many warnings. If something was going to happen, it would have just happened. But no location is worth endangering everyone's safety. I was glad to get out."

Released in 1983, *The Year of Living Dangerously* was a critical success with both mainstream audiences and the art-house crowd and a financial hit. Weaver said of her costar: "He's the most gorgeous man I've ever seen." Hollywood agreed; Gibson had sex appeal, but more significantly, he had a star quality that was bankable. He was quickly tapped to make his American film debut in the Mark Rydell rural drama *The River*, which was scheduled to begin shooting soon.

But first Gibson had another film commitment to fulfill before he could finally go to Hollywood. During that film's making, however, Mad Mel's offscreen escapades would earn him scandalous headlines; eventually, he would land in a pack of personal trouble and jeopardize his career.

Popularized by Charles Nordhoff and James Norman Hall's 1933 novel *Mutiny on the Bounty*, the historic confrontation between Fletcher Christian and Captain Bligh, which resulted in mutiny, had been the subject of four feature films: a 1916 Australian silent called *Mutiny of the Bounty*; a 1933 New Zealand film, *In the Wake of the Bounty*, starring a young Errol Flynn; and

the two most famous versions, made in 1935 and 1962.

Following the stinging reviews and disappointing box office of *Ryan's Daughter,* his epic 1970 love story, David Lean, the distinguished director of such classics as *The Bridge on the River Kwai* (1957), *Lawrence of Arabia* (1962), and *Doctor Zhivago* (1965), decided to have a go at a fifth version after reading a revisionist account of the mutiny called *Captain Bligh and Mr. Christian* by Richard Hough.

Published in 1972, the book cast a very different light on the mutiny and on its two main characters. Although described by Nordhoff and Hall as a brutal, even sadistic, tyrant—and played that way in the 1935 and 1962 films by Charles Laughton and Trevor Howard, respectively—in Hough's book Bligh is a stern but fair-minded disciplinarian as well as an honorable servant in His Majesty's navy.

Traditionally viewed as the hero of the piece, the loyal first mate who could no longer stomach Bligh's atrocities and rebelled against them, Fletcher Christian was described by Hough as a callow youth who "went native" when exposed to the allure of the South Seas and mutinied rather than have to return to England. In an effort to avoid prosecution for his crime under maritime law, Christian sentenced Bligh and those loyal to the captain to certain death by casting them adrift in a small boat so that the crime would never be revealed. But Bligh and his men survived; he returned to England and was declared a hero, while Christian and his followers became hunted men for the rest of their lives, settling on uncharted Pitcairn Island, where all but one of them died before being tracked down by the "long arm of the law."

Determined to tell the true story of the mutiny and its aftermath, which he believed was even more exciting than Nordhoff and Hall's fictionalized account, Lean, in his epic manner, envisioned making two films. The first, to be titled *The Lawbreakers,* would deal with the mutiny; the second film, to be called *The Long Arm,* would chronicle the aftermath. He commissioned Robert Bolt, his writer on *Lawrence, Zhivago,* and *Ryan's Daughter,* to do the screenplays for both films. Meanwhile, Lean, believing he had a deal with producer Dino De Laurentiis, involved himself in preproduction duties—among them the construction of a replica of the actual *Bounty.*

Bolt completed the two scripts, which Lean—and many others who read them—judged "masterful." But the exorbitant cost of making two big-budget epics prompted even the high-rolling De Laurentiis to get skittish; he insisted that the scripts be combined and one film made instead. Bolt did so, but Lean, who had given years to the ambitious project, eventually dropped out for a number of reasons, and the single script was made in 1984 as *The Bounty,* directed by New Zealander Roger Donaldson.

Mel Gibson was cast as Fletcher Christian; Anthony Hopkins, as Bligh. Interestingly, Hopkins headed the short list of actors Lean himself had in mind for the role. Gibson had not yet established a name when Lean was involved, so it's pure speculation as to whether Lean would have chosen him for the role of Fletcher Christian had he made the film in 1984 instead of Donaldson. But it's not inconceivable; Gibson was perfect for the part.

The Bounty earned mixed reviews and was a box-office flop, which inspired more headlines during its making than afterward due to Gibson's off-set behavior.

Always a heavy drinker, the young star's consumption of alcohol (mostly beer) during the film's lengthy shoot in French Polynesia and New Zealand got even heavier. Accounts of Gibson's benders and barroom brawls raged through the press, the bad publicity jarring the nerves of the Hollywood executives who were about to give him his first big break in America in *The River,* where he was cast as an upstanding Tennessee farmer.

But Gibson towed the line, got the break to make *The River,* and the negative headlines subsided—only to resurface worse than ever during the making of his next Hollywood-financed film, *Mrs. Soffel* (1984), a love story about a warden's wife (Diane Keaton) who falls for a prisoner (Gibson), which was shot after but released before *The River.* The film, directed

With Tina Turner in Mad Max: Beyond Thunderdome, *Gibson's least favorite of the* Mad Max *films. After it, he took a two-year sabbatical from the screen.*

by Aussie Gillian Armstrong, was shot in Toronto, where Gibson hit the bottle again, got involved in a car accident, and was arrested for drunk driving.

The press reported the incident gleefully, saying the actor was drowning his promising career in booze. His wife, as well as many of his friends and closest associates, thought so, too. But despite efforts to quit, his drinking continued unabated during the making of his next film, the third (and, to date, last) installment in the *Mad Max* series, *Mad Max Beyond Thunderdome* (1985).

Boozing it up royally when not shooting, Gibson gave interviews to the press in which he was quoted as calling the film lousy and a waste of his time. The quotes were reported worldwide, not exactly endearing him to the film's backers, Warner Bros. Critics bashing your film was one thing, but hearing your star do it was another. The budget for the film was considerable, and they could see their investment threatened.

Despite Gibson's alleged drunken pronouncements on the film's artistic qualities (or lack thereof), *Mad Max Beyond Thunderdome* was

drank so much, I'd surprise even myself. Some mornings I'd wake up with no idea where the hell I'd *been* the night before."

After finishing *Mad Max Beyond Thunderdome,* Gibson bought a large ranch in Australia and settled his family there. (He later bought a house in Malibu, a spread in Montana, and a mansion in Greenwich, Connecticut, not far from his "upstate" New York roots.) He also decided to take some time off from filmmaking in an effort to get his head together and his drinking problem under control.

By 1990, however, he knew he couldn't control it. After another drunken escapade with several women in a Modesto, California, bar, where he was unwinding from an exhausting promotional tour for *Hamlet,* hit the tabloid headlines, he realized there was no other alternative. His doctor told him he might have liver damage and had to stop drinking altogether—and with the help of Alcoholics Anonymous, he has managed to do so.

While Gibson was resting up from the rigors of *Mad Max Beyond Thunderdome* on his cattle ranch in Australia, scripts continued to pour in to the rising star, who now commanded more than $1 million per picture. But Gibson turned them all down. Then a script called *Lethal Weapon* arrived on his desk from his agent.

The script was written by a twenty-four-year-old screenwriting newcomer named Shane Black, whose only previous credit was a low-budget horror movie called *The Monster Squad* (1987). The script was considered such a hot property that a bidding war ensued. Warner Bros. and director Richard Donner won out, and Black was paid a huge sum for his script, ushering in the era of big bucks for tyro screenwriters who came up with a high-concept script.

Lethal Weapon was pure high concept. Its plot could be summed up in a sentence: Young cop at the end of his rope teams with older cop at the end of his career to nail a bunch of former Vietnam vets turned violent drug dealers. The hero, Martin Riggs, distraught over the violent death of his wife, no longer cares

a hit. It also marked a turning point for Gibson by making him face up to his drinking problem, which had been exacerbated by the relentless schedule of shooting four major films virtually back-to-back without a breather.

He has been quite candid about this period in his life and the drinking problem that plagued it. "I'd been a heavy boozer since I was sixteen," he told writer Wensley Clarkson. "In Australia, you're not considered a proper man unless you drink yourself stupid. I was a real hard case, a wild boy, knocking liquor back like there was no tomorrow. I fought so hard and whether he lives or dies. In pursuit of the bad guys, he places himself and his reluctant partner in constant jeopardy with reckless abandon.

The role appealed to Gibson as a variation on his Mad Max character, for while Max also lost a wife to violence, he *did* care whether he survived his near-death adventures on the road and in the arena. Riggs was a virtual psychotic in his grief; in the character's suicidal pain, Gibson saw an opportunity to turn the part into another lead role–cum-character part.

Lethal Weapon hit box-office pay dirt, amassing more than $65 million in the United States alone, where it was the top-grossing film of 1987. It was so successful that it inevitably spawned a sequel. Typically, a sequel tends to earn less than the film that spawned it. In this case, however, *Lethal Weapon 2* more than doubled the take of its predecessor, a whopping $147,254,000 in domestic rentals, and was the top-grossing film of 1989. *Lethal Weapon 3*, which appeared three years later, did almost as well, earning a substantial $144,721,000, which made it the top-grossing film of 1993. Each sequel grew progressively more cartoonlike, with Gibson pushing the Riggs character in an increasingly zany direction: the hero-as-heart-throb version of the Three Stooges.

Back on the screen and bankable in a big way, Gibson was next approached by writer-director Robert Towne to star in *Tequila Sunrise* (1988).

One of the most respected screenwriters in Hollywood, Towne had won the Oscar for *Chinatown* (1974) and been nominated two other times, for *The Last Detail* (1973) and *Shampoo* (1975). He'd directed only one film, the critical favorite but financially disappointing *Personal Best* (1982). *Tequila Sunrise* was to be his second stab at directing, and he'd been shopping the script around for almost six years. At one point, Harrison Ford was onboard, but the superstar ultimately balked at playing a drug dealer, even one who is trying to go straight, the part eventually played by Mel Gibson.

Gibson says he fell for the script immediately. ("You don't read them like that every day.") The dark shadings Towne had given the character were precisely what attracted Gibson to the role. It was another opportunity to play a leading role with blemishes that was, in essence, a character part. The film was only a modest success, however.

Gibson moved from the relatively low key mayhem of *Tequila Sunrise* (1988), which was more drama than action pic, into a series of action-comedies, the first being *Lethal Weapon 2* (1989). It was followed in quick succession by *Air America* and *Bird on a Wire* (both 1990).

Air America was a *M*A*S*H*-like black comedy about CIA-backed pilots running arms and drugs into Laos during the Vietnam War. The script had been kicking around Hollywood for a while. Richard Rush penned the earliest drafts based on a book of the same title by British journalist Christopher Robbins. Rush was set to direct the picture as well. But he eventually dropped out of the project due to creative differences with producer Daniel Melnick, and director Bob Rafelson (*Five Easy Pieces*) hopped aboard instead.

John Eskow was hired to have another go at Rush's script, which Melnick and Rafelson both felt should emphasize the comedy rather than the blackness of the pilots' airborne adventures. But a Writers Guild strike intervened. By the time it was settled and Eskow could get to work, Rafelson was off on another project and editor-turned-director Roger Spottiswoode was now in charge. He encouraged Eskow to lighten the film's tone even more.

The film was shot in Thailand amid monsoons, earthquakes, and other forces of nature that seemed bent on slowing production to a crawl, if not shutting it down outright. In the film, Gibson plays a pilot for the covert operation who "goes native," like Fletcher Christian. Robert Downey Jr. is his younger, more idealistic sidekick. The film's madcap comedy occasionally turns dramatic, but never black.

Robbins, whose book was an exposé of the Air America operation that raised serious questions about the CIA's involvement in the Vietnam War, was indignant when he saw the broad comedy his work had been transformed into on the screen. He expressed his anger in the press. "A hundred thousand people were killed because of Air America's atrocities," he said.

Danny Glover as Murtaugh and Mel Gibson as Riggs, the Larry and Moe (and sometimes Curly, too) of the action-thriller genre.

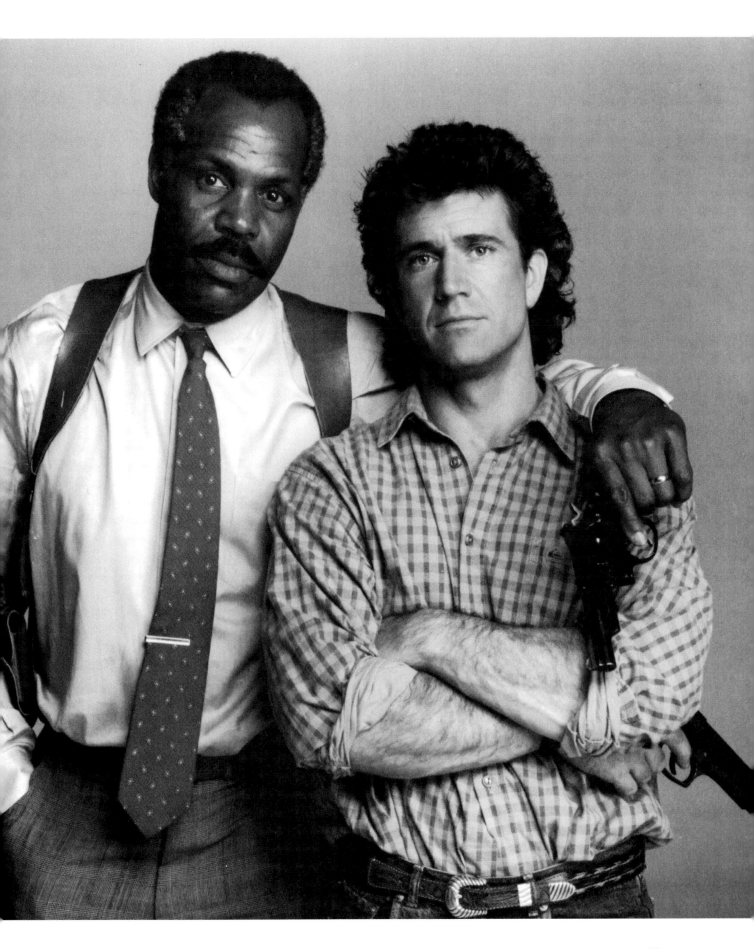

With writer-director Robert Towne on the set of Tequila Sunrise.

"The film is a very trivial comedy about a tragedy." In the United States, *Air America* earned back only $31,054,000 of its $35-million budget.

No less trivial, but not about a tragedy, was Gibson's next action-comedy, *Bird on a Wire*. In it he plays a man in the government's Witness Protection Program whose whereabouts are discovered by the drug dealers he's got the goods on; he escapes and goes mirthfully on the lam, reluctantly helped by his ex-girlfriend (Goldie Hawn), with the killers in high pyrotechnic pursuit.

The film was just a high-concept vehicle for its two popular, high-priced stars. Gibson was not oblivious to the venture's light weight; he called it just a harmless, "frothy piece of action and fun." Audiences agreed; while often reported as being a commercial failure, the film took in more than $70 million at the box office.

Unlike some of his other action-comedies, however, *Bird on a Wire* offered Gibson no opportunity to play his leading-man role as anything but a leading man. It did make him richer, though. His salary for the picture was $4.5 million plus a percentage of the profits, and the film's success, while not in the *Lethal Weapon 2* league, was substantial enough to add to his box-office luster and enable him to take a risk with his next film by taking on the most complex role in all literature.

"Being a star," Mel Gibson has said, "is being a target. It's like having your pants down around your ankles and your hands tied behind your back. You become a good opportunity for some parasite to throw darts in your chest."

Old flames whose romance is reignited during a cross-country run for their lives: Mel and Goldie in Bird on a Wire.

When it was announced that Gibson had agreed to play the title role in a new screen version of Shakespeare's *Hamlet* for Italian director Franco Zeffirelli, the parasites showed up with the darts even before the cameras started to roll. "Hunk Plays Hamlet!" headlines jeered, the reviews already in.

It was a daring career gamble for the action star of the *Mad Max* and *Lethal Weapon* series—hardly, one might think, the sort of training ground to prepare an actor for the clas-

Inviting the critics' scorn by accepting the role, Gibson gave the part of Hamlet "everything I had."

sics. But Zeffirelli didn't agree. In fact, it was one of Gibson's scenes in the first *Lethal Weapon* movie that caused the director to believe that Gibson would make an ideal *Hamlet* and prompted him to approach the actor in the first place.

The scene (the most memorable in the movie) is the one in which the despairing Riggs contemplates suicide. The mixture of tears, terror, determination, ambivalence, and indecision Gibson brought to the scene mirrored Hamlet's own strung-out moment of truth in the famous "To be or not to be" soliloquy. The scene was electric, and so was Gibson. *This*, Zef-

Robert Downey Jr. and Mel Gibson played daredevil pilots in Air America, *a black comedy about covert CIA operations in Laos during the Vietnam War.*

firelli felt, was exactly the Hamlet he'd envisioned for a film since playing the role himself in a student production and later directing the play onstage. The only question was whether Gibson would be game enough to risk his career fortunes on the slings and arrows of outraged critics and skeptical audiences by accepting the role.

The idea had several things going for it. The first was Zeffirelli himself. He had a proven track record of translating Shakespeare successfully to the screen. His *Taming of the Shrew* (1967), with Richard Burton and Elizabeth

As Daniel, the test pilot–hero of the romantic-fantasy Forever Young. *Gibson wanted to make a film he could take his kids to.*

30

Taylor, was a critical and box-office winner. And his youth-oriented *Romeo and Juliet* (1968), with unknowns Leonard Whiting and Olivia Hussey, not only got excellent reviews but was, for its time, a blockbuster, even packing in the teeny-bopper crowd, which normally doesn't go near anything connected to Shakespeare with a ten-foot pole. He wanted his *Hamlet* to reach out to the new generation of teens and their elders and needed a star with Gibson's crossover appeal to achieve this, not to mention attract

the backing to get the film made.

The second thing the idea had going for it was that Gibson was not put off by the challenge of undertaking Shakespeare. He'd already done it as a student at the NIDA and professionally early on in his stage career. He'd never played Hamlet, though, and that, perhaps, was what sold him. If you're an actor, turning down the invitation to play what is widely believed to be the greatest role for an actor in the English language bordered on professional cowardice.

The third thing was that Gibson would be surrounded by a top-flight cast: Glenn Close as Hamlet's adulteress mother, Queen Gertrude; Helena Bonham Carter as the doomed Ophe-

Nick Stahl as student Chuck Norstadt and Mel Gibson as his teacher and mentor Justin McLeod in The Man Without a Face.

As the lonely, disfigured outcast of The Man Without a Face. *In many ways, the film was Gibson's reflection on the slings and arrows of movie stardom, a call for critics and audiences to look beyond surface appearances.*

lia; Ian Holm as Polonius; and two former stage Hamlets, Alan Bates and Paul Scofield, as King Claudius and the ghost of Hamlet's slain father, respectively.

So Gibson signed on to the venture, taking a fraction of his star's salary (now up to almost $10 million a picture) in exchange for a percentage of the film's profits. This was done to keep production costs low and to facilitate financing. The film was modestly budgeted at $15.5 million, a good chunk of that coming from Gibson's own newly formed production company, Icon Productions, when potential

backers balked at the profitability of doing Shakespeare, Gibson's name notwithstanding.

The picture was shot in various castles on the east coast of Scotland and the southern coast of England over a seventy-day period, beginning on April 23, 1990, and ending on July 2, 1990. To prepare for the role, Gibson studied with a voice coach to achieve a believable English accent. He also read the play numerous times in an effort to ferret out every contradictory nuance of the part—a character role with lead billing.

In the end, he said, "Figurin' Hamlet is like lookin' for Bigfoot. I just played him the way I saw him. He's a man of action who can't act [as Zeffirelli envisioned]. I gave it everything I had. What isn't there wasn't in me."

What *was* there surprised just about every-

Gibson moved behind the camera to direct and star in The Man Without a Face. *"If I was going to direct another film, I would not act in it," he vowed, finding the dual responsibilities exhausting.*

Flanked by Jodie Foster and James Garner in Maverick, *a big-screen version of the classic TV show that had starred Garner.*

one, his daunting costars especially, including those who'd played the difficult role themselves. Alan Bates called Gibson's performance "wonderful."

As expected, there were some detractors among the reviewer-parasites waiting eagerly with their darts. But on the whole, *Hamlet* was both a

personal and professional triumph for Mel Gibson, although, in his typically self-deprecating manner, he says of his work in the film: "It was okay. We didn't disgrace ourselves exactly."

Mel Gibson followed the heavyweight challenge of playing *Hamlet* with *Forever Young*

(1992), a lightweight romantic fantasy in the vein of the 1943 tearjerker *A Guy Named Joe* (and Steven Spielberg's 1989 *Always,* a remake of that tear-jerker).

Gibson says he undertook the project for two reasons. One was the challenge of testing his acting mettle by working with kids, in defiance of the axiom that actors should avoid working with kids and dogs at all costs to avoid being upstaged.

The second reason was that he wanted to make a film that would not only appeal to but be appropriate for younger audiences; most of his films up to this time were rated R (no one under seventeen admitted without parent or guardian), including the hugely popular *Lethal Weapon* movies, which Gibson wouldn't allow even his own kids to see because of the films' mayhem and violence, cartoonlike though it is. *Forever Young* was rated PG.

Forever Young is about growing up, about reaching maturity and facing responsibility without sacrificing the sense of wonder, idealism, and brio in that kid you once were. It's a theme intrinsic to many of Gibson's films, especially his first film as a director, where it is more deeply explored. It seems to resonate with Gibson, who freely admits in interviews that he's just a big kid.

Like many actors, Mel Gibson had always wanted to appear in a western. The trouble was that by the time he entered the movies, the genre had become box-office poison; westerns were no longer being made. Action movies, like Gibson's own *Mad Max* and *Lethal Weapon* series, which borrowed elements from the western and transposed them to a modern, usually urban or futuristic, setting, had replaced them.

The unexpected critical and commercial success of Kevin Costner's epic western *Dances With Wolves* (1990) and Clint Eastwood's grim shoot-'em-up *Unforgiven* (1992) briefly revived the moribund genre, however. Other westerns were quickly rushed into production by producers hungry to strike box-office lightning themselves. Instead of coming up with fresh material or a fresh approach to the genre that might push it in a dramatic new direction and give it legs, they just trotted out the familiar legends of Billy the Kid, Wyatt Earp, and Geron-imo that had been filmed hundreds of times before. Or they turned to the small screen for material that was equally familiar and might be successfully translated to the big screen.

One of the most well known and fondly remembered TV westerns of all was *Maverick,* which aired on ABC from 1957 to 1962. It starred James Garner as Bret Maverick, a sly, sometimes larcenous, gambler who preferred card games and con games over gunplay. Though skilled with a six-gun, Maverick was, in fact, "gun-shy" (the title of one of the series most memorable episodes, a parody of TV's *Gunsmoke*), and relied on his wits to get him out of scrapes. The series was as much a comedy as it was a western.

Maverick's combination of action and laughs struck executives at Warner Bros., the studio that produced the original series, as sure-fire box office, and veteran screenwriter William Goldman was commissioned to produce a script for a theatrical version that would attract an all-star cast. The script he wrote, which combined the hoodwinking tone of *The Sting* (1973) with the contemporary touch of his own satiric western *Butch Cassidy and the Sundance Kid* (1969), both starring Paul Newman, had that appeal. Newman himself was courted to play Zane Cooper, Maverick's cardsharp-nemesis in the corkscrew plot, who turns out to be Maverick's pappy and in cahoots with him. Meg Ryan was on the A-list to play the swindling Annabelle, Maverick's female counterpart and love interest, a role that may have been inspired by Diane Brewster's Samantha Crawford character in the original series.

Mel Gibson was the unanimous choice of the executives to play Maverick, and when offered the part, he jumped at it. Here at last was his opportunity to do a western that was right up his alley—a zany one in which the comic side of his screen persona could cut loose big-time.

Richard Donner was signed to direct; he seemed the ideal choice. Not only was he an old hand at guiding Gibson in action-comedies (the *Lethal Weapon* movies); he had actually directed numerous TV westerns early on in his career, although *Maverick* wasn't one of them.

Eventually, Ryan and Newman fell by the wayside. Their roles went to Jodie Foster and

TV's original Maverick, James Garner, whom Gibson lobbied personally to play the part of Cooper, which grew from a glorified cameo into a costarring one largely because of Garner's adroitness with the material. Many, including Mel Gibson himself, believe Garner was so good in the role that he stole the show out from under his younger costars.

Throughout shooting, Gibson was constantly worried about his own performance, that he was overdoing the comic shenanigans and lapsing too much into shtick. He turned out to be right. Audiences didn't seem to mind, however. The film was a big hit, though it did little for the cause of the western, which has since returned to the dead, or yet another long sleep.

"Gibson sings!" While perhaps not as eagerly anticipated as "Garbo talks!" this announcement created sufficient excitement across the pop-culture landscape to propel the Disney organization's animated musical *Pocahontas* to

As Bret Maverick. Gibson had long wanted to make a western.

the top of the box-office heap in 1995.

Although Mel Gibson had warbled a tune in *Maverick*, his onscreen singing credentials were virtually nil. But this didn't discourage Disney executives from approaching him to play the part of Capt. John Smith in the studio's cartoon version of the love affair between the legendary Native American princess and the English explorer of seventeenth-century Virginia. On the contrary, Gibson's distinctive speaking voice and marquee value were credentials enough. Hadn't Rex Harrison and Richard Burton successfully acquitted themselves in musicals without being able to sing a note?

Always up for a challenge, Gibson, an inveterate "shower singer," he says, signed on with little persuasion. After all, what was singing a couple of songs in a movie in which your face

Directing, in costume, the Battle of Stirling for Braveheart. *He wanted the audience to "get the smell" of thirteenth-century warfare.*

never appears compared to the risk of playing Hamlet front and center?

As with *Hamlet,* in which he had worked extensively with a dialect coach to perfect a credible English accent, Gibson prepared for his offscreen singing debut in *Pocahontas* by spending long hours with a Disney voice coach to hone his ability to carry a tune. Had be been unable to, someone else would have been brought in to sing the part of John Smith, although Gibson would continue to speak it, as was the case with *Pocahontas* herself: Irene Bedard spoke the dialogue, but Judy Kuhn did the singing.

But according to one Disney executive, Gibson evidenced a natural ability from the start. Everyone breathed a sign of relief (the film's ballyhoo could now indeed trumpet "Gibson sings!" across the land), including the star himself, who says he enjoyed the experience of participating in a musical but adds that he is not inclined to repeat it.

In the movie, he sings no solos, but belts out several duets with David Ogden Stiers and others. The film again reunited him with his *Year of Living Dangerously* costar Linda Hunt, who had a cameo in *Maverick* and voices the role of Grandmother Willow in *Pocahontas.*

Gibson rounded out the year by appearing on-screen, albeit briefly, in a much less challenging role. He played himself in a cameo appearance in *Casper* (1995), a special effects blowout combining live action and computer generated animation, based on the famous comic strip about everybody's favorite friendly ghost.

Much later, he appeared in another uncredited role in the Robin Williams–Billy Crystal comedy *Father's Day* (1997), where he played a character almost as dim as Scollop in *Summer City,* whose obsession is not surfing, but earrings.

In between all these cinematic activities, Mel Gibson the actor also moved behind the camera to direct his first film.

Directing. It's not uncommon these days for movie stars with clout to want to try their hands at it. They may believe that because they are actors themselves, they are more in tune with the needs of actors and thus can do a better job of directing than those nonactors who've been guiding their screen performances. Or they may come across a project they fall so much in love with that acting in it isn't enough; they feel they must call *all* the shots to make sure that the project is fully realized the way they envision it. Directing films (in tandem with producing them) is also a way of ensuring that an actor gets the parts he or she craves rather than waiting for them to be offered.

All these considerations were uppermost in Mel Gibson's mind when he formed Icon Productions, in 1990, with Australian accountant Bruce Davey. Together they financed Zeffirelli's *Hamlet,* a film that might never have gotten off the ground without Icon's support.

Gibson told the press that he formed Icon in order to make quality films with something to say: "There's got to be more to this business than 'popcorn munching.' " The company was set up to produce films in which Gibson would star *(Hamlet, Forever Young, The Man Without a Face, Maverick, Braveheart)* as well as quality films by other directors, such as Bernard Rose's 1994 Beethoven biopic *Immortal Beloved,* in which Gibson would not appear. But its primary objective was to serve as a launch pad for Gibson's own directorial career, one that would involve projects of his own choosing.

Because of his power in the industry, Gibson had had opportunities to direct before, but the offers were for films in the action-comedy vein of *Lethal Weapon,* which had made him a star. He wanted to surprise people by making his directorial debut with something very different. And Isabelle Holland's novel *The Man Without a Face,* the story of a lonely, disfigured outcast and the lonely, fatherless boy he teaches to look beyond surface appearances, was, for him, the perfect subject.

Shot in various parts of coastal Maine and at Bowdoin College, north of Portland, the film is Gibson's very personal take on the theme of growing up and assuming responsibility. In many ways it is also the actor's reflection on the vicissitudes of movie stardom—a repudiation of the superficial "sexiest man alive" image that

As William Wallace in Braveheart. *The script was pitched to him to star in, but after reading it, he knew he had to direct the film as well.*

With pal Jodie Foster at the Golden Globe Awards, where the accolades for Braveheart *started coming in.*

has dogged him throughout his career and a call for critics and audiences to look beneath the handsome face and take him seriously as the versatile and creative talent many of his films, most recently *Hamlet,* showed him to be.

Befitting Gibson's sensibilities, the film is not heavy or humorless (the Bergmanesque approach to being taken seriously of actor-directors like Woody Allen), but it *is* a drama. Symbolic of the point Gibson is trying to make, he conceals his celebrated looks behind grue-some scar makeup (the character was disfigured in a car crash) in an effort to make the audi-ence forget he *is* Mel Gibson. In doing so, he also gives the part the trademark Gibson twist, turning it into a character role even though it is a lead.

A modest film, *The Man Without a Face* was a modest success that earned $24,753,227 at the box office domestically (more worldwide) and mild praise from the critics, who applauded the deft and unexpectedly moving storytelling skills of the action star turned novice director. Like *Hamlet, The Man Without a Face* (1993) was a personal triumph for Gibson, and, as with *Hamlet,* he underplayed his achievement by saying that at least he hadn't disgraced himself. He confessed to the press, however, that direct-ing was more of a challenge than he'd antici-pated, "especially if you're directing yourself. If I was going to direct another film, I would not act in it." But when that time came, he went back on his word because the part was just too good to pass up.

Randall Wallace's script *Braveheart,* the story of a thirteenth-century Scottish clansman's war for liberty against England's ruthless King Edward I, was submitted to Icon Productions in the hopes of getting a commitment from Gibson to star. But after reading the script, Gibson felt he had to *tell* the story as well, for he kept reworking scenes from it in his head. "That's a pretty good indication you should probably direct it, if you're building images and sequences in your head," he revealed in a promotional film for the movie.

A lover of films since his youth, Gibson had a special affinity for what he calls "the *big* ones like *The Big Country,* that western, and *Spartacus,* the huge, epic films. They were what inspired me to do *Braveheart.*" To overcome the many pressures of mounting such a complex production and wearing so many hats, Gibson took to walking about the sets with a book in

his hand bearing the gag title "A Beginner's Guide to Directing the Epic."

What inspired him to make the film also was the character the script was about, a somewhat obscure Scottish national hero named William Wallace (no relation to screenwriter, Randall Wallace, as far as the latter knows). "[William] Wallace was truly interested in liberty and loved his country and really wanted to be free and wanted freedom for his fellows," Gibson said. "But at the same time, he was kind of a savage. At the Battle of Stirling, he skinned the commanding officer on the other side and turned him into a belt." The part of Wallace was the lead, but a character role as well, one that would stretch the audience's support and thus tailor-made for the star.

Wallace's rage against the British tyrants was motivated as well by their murder of his wife. This prompted Gibson to wryly start call-

Gibson both sang and spoke the role of Capt. John Smith in Disney's animated musical Pocahontas.

ing the character "Mad Mac;" Mad Max's call to arms was motivated by a similar tragedy.

Budgeted at $55.5 million (with Gibson again taking a fraction of his then $15-million-per-picture superstar's salary to get the film made), *Braveheart* (1995) was shot in Scotland and Ireland with a cast of what looks on the screen like thousands, even though it isn't. Extras for the enormous battle scenes were conscripted from Ireland's army reserve forces due to the need for extras who were not only disciplined in functioning like an army but physically up to the film's rigorous and dangerous stunt work.

While the battle scenes are not the sum and substance of *Braveheart,* they rank among the film's most memorable set pieces because of their extraordinary staging and uncompromisingly vivid brutality. This is especially true of the film's major battle scene on the plains of Stirling, where Wallace and his band of savages successfully defeated the English forces. The scene took six weeks to shoot.

To prepare for it, Gibson says he looked at all the great battle scenes in films he could lay his hands on—films such as *Spartacus* (1960) and Orson Welles's *Chimes at Midnight* (1967). "[I wanted] to see the kind of territory that's been covered and then go further with it," he said, "and really get the feeling of what it must

As paranoid New York City cabdriver Jerry Fletcher, the man who knows too much, in Conspiracy Theory *(1997).*

be like to be in the middle of a thirteenth-century battle. To get the *smell* of it."

He captured more than the smell of it; before submitting the film to the Motion Picture Association of America (MPAA) for classification, he toned down the graphic bloodshed both to avoid an NC-17 rating and not gross audiences out. "I didn't really know [how gory the film was] until I showed it to an audience and they were going for the vomit bags and getting up and walking out," he told an interviewer after the film's release. "You don't want that; you want people to stay with it."

What he wanted most was for moviegoers to be so moved by the film emotionally that they couldn't talk after the lights went up. "I hope that they're so moved and so . . . *inspired* by it, that's all," he said. "That they've watched this great story and they've found something in themselves."

Released early in 1995 to high commercial expectations, given Gibson's following and the fact that the film was both a love story and an action epic, *Braveheart* initially performed below these expectations at the box office. But it had legs. It would move out of one theater, to be replaced by the next hot new release, only to move to another one or return to the same theater later for a second run. Word of mouth steadily built, and by the end of the year the film had become a hit, albeit not one of that year's, or Gibson's, biggest.

Braveheart received numerous awards, including the Golden Globe (for Best Picture) for Gibson, a foreshadowing of things to come when the Oscar nominations were announced in February 1996. The film received multiple nominations, including Best Director and Best Picture. When the envelopes were opened at the Academy Awards ceremony that April, Gibson's name and *Braveheart* were inside.

In his acceptance speech for the directing award, Gibson offered the customary thank-yous to family, friends, and collaborators. Then he went on to express his thanks to every director he ever worked with. "They were my film school," he added, then observing wryly, "and now that I'm a bona fide director with a golden boy, I, well, like most directors, I suppose what I really want to do is act." The remark brought the house down, though it is my belief that what most directors really, *really,* want to do is write.

Gibson was kidding; it's doubtful he'll never move behind the cameras into the director's chair again, for *Braveheart* was not just the work of another big-name actor dabbling in directing but of an actor with directing in his blood.

By 1996, Mel Gibson's asking price per film had skyrocketed to $20 million, placing him in the top salary tier of male superstars like Arnold Schwarzenegger, Sylvester Stallone, and Tom Hanks. Producers feel the price is a bargain, given the collective box-office receipts of Gibson's films worldwide. For a long time, he had had his choice of roles and could be very choosy about them—but now even more so.

Gibson turned down the lead part of dapper John Steed in a planned big-screen version of the classic TV spy-spoof series *The Avengers,* feeling neither suited for the part nor interested in it, for the character of Steed lacked the qualities he looks for in a lead role. Earlier, he had been in the running to be the new James Bond after Roger Moore left the series and on the A-list again when Timothy Dalton was unceremoniously dumped after two post-Moore Bond films. But he turned the lucrative Bond offers down each time for the same reasons he'd rejected playing John Steed.

Instead, he elected to make his debut as a $20 million megastar in Ron Howard's *Ransom* (1996). The film was a remake of the 1956 film of the same name which had starred Glenn Ford and Donna Reed as parents whose son is kidnapped after which the father places a bounty on the kidnapper's heads to get the boy back. Ironically, the script of the earlier film had been cowritten by Richard Maibaum, chief scriptwriter of numerous James Bond films. The new version was updated by Alexander Ignon and novelist-screenwriter Richard Price, with Mel Gibson and René Russo taking the Ford and Reed roles.

Gibson says he decided to take the role of the desperate father in *Ransom* because the character shared the weaknesses and vulnerabilities of Mad Max and even William Wallace, who are similarly spurred to action when confronted by an act of violence against their families. Unlike them, however, Tom Mullen, Gibson's family man turned avenger, is neither a superhero nor a larger-than-life figure, though he is rich and powerful, which makes his initial helplessness in the tense situation all the more difficult for him to deal with. In fact, worrying the character might appear too competent and thus lose audience identification, Gibson urged screenwriter Richard Price to play down Mullen's self-confidence and play up his self-doubt even more in subsequent drafts. "To me, it's interesting to see him [Mullen] in a corner biting the chair," the actor told *Cinescape* magazine.

The point where Mullen finally decides to stop biting the chair, get out of the corner, and cut loose on his own to get his son back is intended to be even more electrifying and audience involving precisely because of the character's carefully etched feelings of helplessness and uncertainty. In many ways it mirrors the moment when Fletcher Christian at last erupts against Captain Bligh in *The Bounty*—and for many of the same reasons.

Gibson also had a hand in writing some of the script himself. Perhaps inspired by a similar sequence in the Clint Eastwood action movie *Dirty Harry*, Gibson and an assistant came up with a lengthy chase scene in which the kidnapper puts Gibson's stressed-out character through a rigorous workout, sending him from one spot to another during the ransom drop and forcing him to reach each spot in record time—or else.

Ransom provided Mel Gibson a welcome break from the demanding responsibilities of being both before and behind the cameras. Not that just simply appearing in the film was free of difficulties. To make the action scenes look real, Gibson had to perform numerous, and dangerous, stunts himself, ranging from sidestepping treacherous New York City traffic to jumping over taxicab hoods. Behind the scenes, he also suffered a headlined bout of appendicitis, which resulted in his being rushed to a New York City hospital for emergency surgery, halting production for a week. For his performance, he received a Golden Globe nomination in the Best Actor In a Drama category, though he didn't take home the prize. (Ironically, the winner, Geoffrey Rush for *Shine*, had

once been a roommate of Gibson's during the superstar's early stage-acting days in Australia.)

Gibson has so far resisted the efforts of Warner Bros. and director Richard Donner to sign him for a fourth installment of the popular *Lethal Weapon* series. *Entertainment Weekly* reported that the studio offered him $25 million to reprise the character of Riggs one more time, while *Variety*, the show-biz Bible, said the offer ran as high as $30 million, a salary that would make Mel Gibson the highest-paid actor in history.

A first-draft script of *Lethal Weapon 4* has been written by Jonathan Lemkin, whose previous credits include the screenplay for the 1993 Sylvestor Stallone actioner *Demolition Man*. Allegedly, it brings back René Russo's Lorna Cole character for another go-around with Gibson's Riggs and Danny Glover's Murtaugh but this time drops Joe Pesci's Leo Getz character. Gibson's agent has said that the actor has not ruled out the prospect of appearing in a *Lethal Weapon 4* and is willing to look at any and all scripts for the vehicle, but Gibson has publicly expressed exhaustion with the character of Riggs and the opinion that the character and the series have been taken about as far as each will go. Danny Glover feels much the same way and has so far also declined to appear in a fourth installment, adding that he's more interested in pursuing other career directions and not repeating himself in a piece of material that has "already been done so well."

I'm inclined to agree. There's little rationale for another *Lethal Weapon* movie apart from the money it would probably make for all concerned. The series has been played out, although director Richard Donner believes there's enough life in it yet for two more sequels.

Keeping true to his word that he just wants to act for a while, Gibson chose to star rather than direct and star in his next film, *Conspiracy Theory*, and turned over the directorial reins to his old pal Donner, with whom the actor has developed a strong personal and professional rapport. Like Gibson, Donner is not inclined to take life too seriously on or off the set, Gibson says, adding that Donner, too, is just a "big kid" at heart.

An action-comedy in the vein of the *Lethal*

Weapon series and thriller in the vein of Alfred Hitchcock's *Man Who Knew Too Much* (1954), with a dash of Hitchcock's *39 Steps* (1935) thrown in for good measure, *Conspiracy Theory* features Gibson as a paranoid New York City cabdriver named Jerry Fletcher who poses endless conspiracy theories over the Internet, one of which, involving a shadow group within the FBI, turns out to be true. With villain Patrick Stewart closing in to silence him, Gibson does a twist on his *Ransom* character and becomes the pursued rather than the pursuer as he runs for his life. Julia Roberts plays the girl on the run with him in the lighthearted adventure.

While making *Conspiracy Theory*, Gibson proposed making a film version of Ray Bradbury's *Fahrenheit 451*, a cautionary science-fiction novel about censorship and book burning that he would both star in and direct. One can see why the book would appeal to him, for its main character, a fireman named Montag who ferrets out books deemed harmful to society by his totalitarian masters and puts them to the torch, has much in common with other Gibson heroes, notably *Braveheart*'s William Wallace. Eventually, the character rebels and becomes an interim leader who enables subsequent generations to preserve their intellectual freedom. Bradbury himself, as well as screenwriters Terry Puryear and Terry K. Hayes, have drafted scripts for the film, which is still in the planning stages.

The novel was filmed once before, in 1967, by director François Truffaut; it starred Julie Christie and Oskar Werner (in the role of Montag). Gibson considers the Truffaut film a missed opportunity and is not alone in calling it "dull and humorless," qualities he hopes to reverse in the remake. Nevertheless, the Truffaut film has since achieved cult status, largely due to its hauntingly beautiful music score by Bernard Herrmann. Gibson would do well to consider reprising Herrmann's score for his remake, as Martin Scorsese did when he remade the 1962 film *Cape Fear* (also scored by Herrmann) in 1991.

Also on Gibson's directing agenda for a brief time was a proposed big-screen remake of the oft-filmed Leo Tolstoy classic *Anna Karenina*, to be made under the banner of Gibson's Icon Productions. Gibson opted not to direct, and the project was shelved while he involved himself in other things (among them *Conspiracy Theory*), then finally green-lighted with Bernard Rose (who had made *Immortal Beloved* for Icon) in the director's chair. French actress Sophie Marceau, Gibson's costar in *Braveheart*, was cast in the title role as Tolstoy's doomed heroine who loves neither too wisely nor too well. The film was released in the spring of 1997.

At press time, two other projects were rumored to be under consideration by Mel Gibson as well.

In one of them, *Enemy of the State*, a thriller to be directed by Tony Scott and produced by Jerry Bruckheimer, Gibson would play a lawyer who becomes a target of the National Security Agency. That would certainly be a challenge for Mel the actor—making us root for a lawyer!

The other, *Thank You for Smoking!*, based on the satiric novel by Christopher Buckley about a cigarette company lobbyist trying to convince people smoking is good for them, has been purchased for filming by Gibson's Icon Productions for him to star in and possibly direct. The subject matter seems ideally suited to the actor's well-known twisted sense of humor, not to mention his sense of irony, given the many public statements he has made about his own difficulties "kicking the habit."

For now it seems that Mel Gibson is, as he has maintained, content to just act for others and be one of the guys on his films rather than guide every stage of production. In fact, this is how Gibson's coworkers—above-the-line talent, technicians, and lowly extras alike—tend to describe him. Whether acting, directing, or being a superstar, they say he *always* comes across as just "one of the guys."

Which is the nature of Mel Gibson's unique and enduring appeal to audiences as well.

Gibson at the Oscars with his two "golden boys" for directing Braveheart *and for Best Picture.*

THE FILMS

SUMMER CITY
(a.k.a. Coast of Terror)

1976—AVALON FILMS

". . . an abomination. A cheap, nasty flick that was cranked out in three weeks."

—MEL GIBSON

CREDITS

Producer: Phil Avalon; *Director:* Christopher Fraser; *Screenwriter:* Phil Avalon; *Cinematographer:* Jerry Marek; *Editor:* David Stiven; *Composer:* Phil Butkis; *Art director:* Jann Harris.
Running time: 89 minutes.

CAST

John Jarratt *(Sandy);* Phil Avalon *(Robbie);* Steve Bisley *(Boo);* Mel Gibson *(Scollop);* Debbie Forman *(Caroline);* James Elliott *(Father);* Abigail *(Girl in Bar).*

REVIEWS

"The film is poorly directed, shoddily photographed and lacks any kind of structure or tension."

—*THE LAST NEW WAVE* (BOOK)

Mel Gibson's first feature film is basically a surfing documentary with the barest bones of a plot strung on it. Phil Avalon, the film's writer, producer, and costar, specialized in surfing documentaries in the vein of American Bruce Brown's *Endless Summer* (1966). *Summer City* appears to have been his attempt to branch out into dramatic features using the same milieu—and much stock footage of gorgeous sunsets and perfect waves left over from his surfing documentaries to pad out the running time.

Four lads head for the coast to enjoy a wild weekend of surfing and boozing and to give one of their group, the soon-to-be-married Jarratt, one last fling before he ties the knot. But Jarratt proves to be a stubborn case; in fact, he's a stick-in-the-mud who resists his mates' every effort to get him to cut loose and have a ball.

When the lads attend a dance near the place where they're lodging, he stays behind to read a book. He is especially scornful of Steve Bisley's character, Boo, an incorrigible womanizer who continually taunts him about settling

Fresh out of acting school, Mel made his inauspicious screen debut in the low budget "beach-buddy" movie Summer City. *He headed straight back to the theater, deciding films were not for him.*

"I'd been goofing off all of my life. I thought I might as well get paid for it," he says of choosing an acting career.

down with one woman. But Gibson's inoffensive surfer-bum Scollop comes in for some jibes as well. "Don't you ever think about what you'll be doing ten years from now?" Jarratt practically sneers. "Probably this," Gibson replies shrugging diffidently.

Jarratt's sermonizing reaches its insufferable peak when Bisley seduces the local virgin, Caroline (Debbie Forman), then dumps her. In tears, she makes the mistake of confiding to Jarratt, who lectures her on the perils of confusing sex with love and recommends she tell all to her father. She does, and the old man goes berserk. He grabs a gun and goes after Bisley, who has taken it on the lam with his mates. Then Jarratt learns that Bisley bedded his fiancée on the eve of their wild weekend and decides to shoot him, too.

The fun-filled weekend climaxes in tragedy when Bisley is finally tracked down by the outraged father and murdered in cold blood. Hunting Bisley with Scollop's rifle, Jarratt sees the killing, and when the father goes after him to silence all witnesses, Jarratt has to shoot him. He is acquitted of murder on grounds of self-defense and takes the train home, where he is met at the station by his unfaithful fiancée, whom he typically scorns at first, though the final fade-out suggests that the two might reconcile, assuming Jarrett ever takes his head out of his "arse."

Summer City was made on an extremely low budget and looks it. It has the appearance of a home movie shot with professional equipment by a bunch of filmmaking hopefuls who haven't yet polished their craft. Scenes meander in a clumsy attempt to reflect the aimless youth lifestyle the film is trying to portray, and individual shots are stretched out to sometimes excruciating length.

The film was by no means in the vanguard of the exciting new wave of Australian films to come in just a few short years, but it isn't quite the abomination Gibson describes it as being, either. The acting is reasonably effective, with particular honors going to Bisley, who has the showiest role, and Forman.

Gibson's role is strictly a supporting one, but because the character is Bisley's sidekick, he gets a substantial amount of screen time. Gibson's slightly dim, surfing-obsessed character Scollop also gets to deliver *Summer City*'s best, and funniest, line.

When the boys' car careens off the road and is totaled, his mates are understandably alarmed and angry at being stranded, but Scollop's only concern is "How far is the beach from here?"

MAD MAX

1979—AMERICAN-INTERNATIONAL PICTURES

"Probably the classiest B-grade trash ever made."
—MEL GIBSON

CREDITS

Producer: Byron Kennedy; *Director:* George Miller;
Screenwriters: George Miller and James McCausland, based
on a story by George Miller and Byron Kennedy;
Cinematographer: David Eggby; *Editors:* Tony Paterson
and Clifford Hayes; *Composer:* Brian May;
Art director: Jon Dowding.
Running time: 93 minutes.

CAST

Mel Gibson *(Max);* Joanne Samuel *(Jessie);* Hugh Keays-
Byrne *(Toecutter);* Steve Bisley *(Jim Goose);* Roger Ward
(Fifi Macaffee); Vincent Gil *(Nightrider);* Tim Burns *(Johnny
Boy);* Geoff Parry *(Bubba Zanetti);* Paul Johnstone
(Cundalini); John Ley *(Charlie);* Jonathan Hardy
(Labatoche); Sheila Florence *(May Swaisey);* Reg Evans
(Stationmaster); Stephen Clark *(Sarse);* Howard Eynon
(Diabando).

REVIEWS

"This is the most audience-involving film since Hal-
loween: *the camera is always on the move, tracking
and craning every which way, while the audience is
never sure where the menace will come from next.
The film belongs to the director, cameraman and
stunt artists: it's not an actor's piece, though the
leads are all effective."*

—VARIETY, 5/16/79

*"Devotees of the 'new' Australian cinema who wish
to keep their illusions intact should give George
Miller's* Mad Max *a miss . . . it looks like a
wretched splicing-together of some of the crasser
notions current in American movies a while back
and now largely, mercifully discarded."*

—NEW STATESMAN, 11/9/79

*"Mad Max is ugly and incoherent, and aimed,
probably accurately, at the most uncritical of moviegoers."*

—NEW YORK TIMES, 6/14/80

Max Rockatansky (Mel Gibson) and his wife, Jessie (Joanne Samuel), enjoy happier times in the postapocalypse action-thriller Mad Max.

Director George Miller first introduces us to his postapocalypse hero Max Rockatansky in a collage of big, bold close-ups—Max's boots, Max's hands, Max's sunglass-covered eyes—to give the character a mythic quality from the get-go, like Clint Eastwood's "man with no name" in the spaghetti westerns of Sergio Leone.

This is just one of many genres and filmmakers to which Miller slyly pays hommage in *Mad Max.* The terrorizing of a small town by some outlaw bikers unmistakably recalls *The Wild One* (1954), though the tone here is infi-

nitely sleazier and more violent. Later, *High Noon* (1952) pops up in an amusing scene in which the bikers collect the body of a dead gang member, telling the stationmaster: "We're here to meet a friend comin' in on the train." The constant chatter over the public-address system in the ramshackle Hall of Justice advising Main Force Patrol (MFP) members of the latest rules, regulations, and restrictions (like not dealing in illicit gasoline) lends the film a satiric quality reminiscent of Robert Altman's

Gibson portrays Max as the essence of leading-man cool.

*M*A*S*H* (1970). Miller says the great silent film comedians like Buster Keaton influenced him as well, and this is reflected in the picture's semislapstick, constantly-on-the-move style.

Among other things, *Mad Max* is a movie made by and for film buffs.

When we finally do get to see the leather-clad Max for the first time, however, Gibson's

Max is an Interceptor for the MFP; it's his job to capture the highway miscreants his colleagues in the MFP's Pursuit units flush out and send his way. The film starts off like a rocket with a kinetic twenty-minute chase scene along a desolate stretch of high-fatality highway called Anarchie Road ("Deaths this year: 57" warn signs along the way).

The pursued is Nightrider (Vincent Gil), a stoned-out member of the Gloryriders gang, headed by a sadistic motorcyclist named Toecutter (played by Hugh Keays-Byrne, who apes Robert Ryan in Sam Peckinpah's *Wild Bunch* by denouncing his cohorts as "scum-sucking trash"). Cars, vans, and motorcycles are smashed to smithereens in the high-velocity melee, which concludes when Max bears down on Nightrider's bumper, sending the outlaw and his moll hurtling into a gasoline truck, to be blown sky-high.

After this stunning opening sequence, the film slows down to acquaint us with Max, his family, and his closest chum on the force, fellow Interceptor Jim Goose (Steve Bisley, Gibson's costar in *Summer City*). The latter keeps drawing Max back into the action despite Max's resolve to go along with his flower child–wife's desire for him to find a safer, less violent line of work.

When Goose is killed by the Gloryriders (they burn him to a crisp by tossing a match on the gas leaking from a tow truck in which Goose is trapped), Max gets spooked, decides he's had enough, and resigns from the force. Knowingly, his commanding officer just grants him a leave of absence. "You'll be back, Max," he says. "You're hooked, and you know it."

The problem is that the commanding officer's insight into Max's character isn't quite as apparent to us. From the outset, Max is portrayed by Gibson as the essence of leading-man cool. In fact, he's almost reserved in his enthusiasm for being a warrior-policeman of the open road. By contrast, his pal Jim Goose is genuinely hot-wired to the adrenaline-pumping lifestyle; there's madness in Goose already, and given the film's title, he seems from the start more like

boyish looks come as a bit of a surprise. The character's whole doesn't quite seem equal to the sum of his parts, not unlike the movie that surrounds him.

The bikers take out their rage on the couple's sedan.

the character we keep expecting Gibson to be.

For audiences seeing *Mad Max* for the first time, the check in which Gibson and/or his director kept the Max character is surprising. Even Max's rage against the Gloryriders when they kill his wife and child is more subdued than expected. Max goes after the bad guys not like some wild-eyed vigilante but in a methodically disciplined, almost detached manner.

Gibson's persona is not yet that of the impulsive man of action who behaves recklessly with little regard for his own or anyone else's safety. The character's adolescent behavior

through much of the film as he clowns with Jim Goose and his other mates on the force is more reminiscent of the character Gibson played in *Summer City,* although Max is intellectually sharper than Scollop and certainly more in control. In fact, unlike the Gibson character of future action films (including the two *Mad Max* sequels), he never seems to lose control or be dangerously out of control. He's always in complete charge of himself, his risk taking always measured.

Max's pursuit of the killers of his family and Jim Goose *is* dogged and ruthless, however.

Closing in on them in the souped-up, 600-horsepower V-8 sedan ("the last of its breed") he swiped from the Hall of Justice garage to be his battlewagon, Max won't give up or back off no matter how outnumbered he is—though he is always careful to calculate the odds. And in the film's final act, in which the flagging plot undergoes a solid jump-start and the action becomes kinetic again, Gibson's Max proves he is no liberal softy when it comes to meting out justice.

No longer the supercool hero, Max is now as cold as ice. In a brutally ironic reprise of Johnny Boy's murder of Jim Goose, he handcuffs Johnny Boy's (Tim Burns) leg to a wreck and torches the dripping gasoline, forcing the man to either sever the limb to survive or die in a fireball. And in the spectacular finale, he uses every torque of his hot V-8 to maneuver the savage Toecutter's motorcycle directly into the path of an oncoming semi, splattering the gang leader all over the road.

Perhaps Gibson's Max in this first installment of the series isn't as "mad" as the title suggests. But by the end of the film he's definitely one pissed-off dude.

No longer just cool but now as cold as ice, Max prepares to give Johnny Boy (Tim Burns) a taste of his own medicine.

TIM

1979—GUO, FILM DISTRIBUTORS

"It's got a lot of rough edges. But it was made with a lot of heart."

—MEL GIBSON

CREDITS

Producer: Michael Pate; *Director:* Michael Pate; *Screenwriter:* Michael Pate, based on the novel by Colleen McCullough; *Cinematographer:* Paul Onorato; *Editor:* David Stiven; *Composer:* Eric Jupp; *Art director:* John Carroll. Running time: 108 minutes.

CAST

Piper Laurie *(Mary Horton);* Mel Gibson *(Tim Melville);* Alwyn Kurts *(Ron Melville);* Pat Evison *(Emily Melville);* Peter Gwynne *(Tom Ainsley);* Deborah Kennedy *(Dawnie Melville);* David Foster *(Mick Harrington);* Margo Lee *(Mrs. Harrington);* James Condon *(Mr. Harrington);* Michael Caulfield *(John Martinson);* Brenda Senders *(Mrs. Parker);* Brian Barrie *(Dr. Perkins);* Kevin Leslie *(Curly Campbell);* Louise Pago *(Secretary);* Arthur Faynes *(Ambulance Attendant).*

REVIEWS

"Mel Gibson . . . gives a good performance as the title character, a backward young man who is befriended and then loved by a compassionate older woman played by Piper Laurie. But this is not the kind of heavyweight stuff the Australian film community is capable of. It's a trifle, though its family scenes are capably directed by Michael Pate."

—CHRISTIAN SCIENCE MONITOR, 8/27/81

" . . . an unintentionally hilarious debacle. It's a gothic romance in reverse—the strong, dominant woman rescues the handsome helpless hunk—and is only noteworthy for Piper Laurie's glowing skin and Mel Gibson's ripe sensuality, which [director] Pate, to my liplicking regret, refrains from developing."

—VILLAGE VOICE, 9/16/81

"Even though Tim *at times lapses into the mawkish, it never loses sight of the importance of allowing Tim to grow up and of its larger sense of the inevitability of change and loss from which not even Tim can be spared.* Tim *is notable not only for these*

Gibson brings a winning ingenuousness to the role of the twenty-four-year-old man-child that captures the audience's heart. He loses himself so convincingly in the part that he doesn't even seem to be acting.

As Mary (Piper Laurie) guides the mentally handicapped Tim in reaching his full potential, their relationship deepens, and they eventually marry.

enlightened sentiments and [sic] for the appeal and persuasiveness of Laurie and Gibson. It's also one of the few films that embraces rather than patronizes ordinary unsophisticated people represented by Tim's parents."

—LOS ANGELES TIMES, 5/8/82

"Gibson plays his part with appropriately benign vacuousness, and Laurie, who eventually—and literally—lets her hair down, reinforces the conviction that she's an attractive woman who deserves better than second-rate Jill Clayburgh."

—NEWSDAY, 9/17/81

Summer City may have given Mel Gibson his first screen break, and *Mad Max* brought him important international exposure in his first megahit, but it was *Tim* that provided him with his best role to date—and offered the first inkling of his star quality. To the role of the twenty-four-year-old man-child of the title who captures the heart of a lonely, middle-aged businesswoman, Gibson brings a winning ingenuousness that captures the audience's heart as well.

The businesswoman is Mary Horton (Piper Laurie), an American who relocated to Australia twenty years earlier. In pursuing her career, she has become "used to not being married" and has resigned herself to spinsterhood. Until she meets Tim.

When her gardener quits, Tim, a good-looking but none-too-bright builder's laborer, is recommended by Mary's neighbor as a substitute, and she hires him. Though standoffish at first, Mary is soon charmed by his boyish manners and earnestness. Touched by his open and honest revelation that he's "not the full quid; anybody'll tell you that" and can neither read nor write, she gives him a children's book, *Wind in the Willows,* and teaches him to read it. She also answers his searching questions about life, death, and other grown-up matters which his overprotective parents, in a mistaken belief he wouldn't understand and in their desire to keep him innocent, have never responded to.

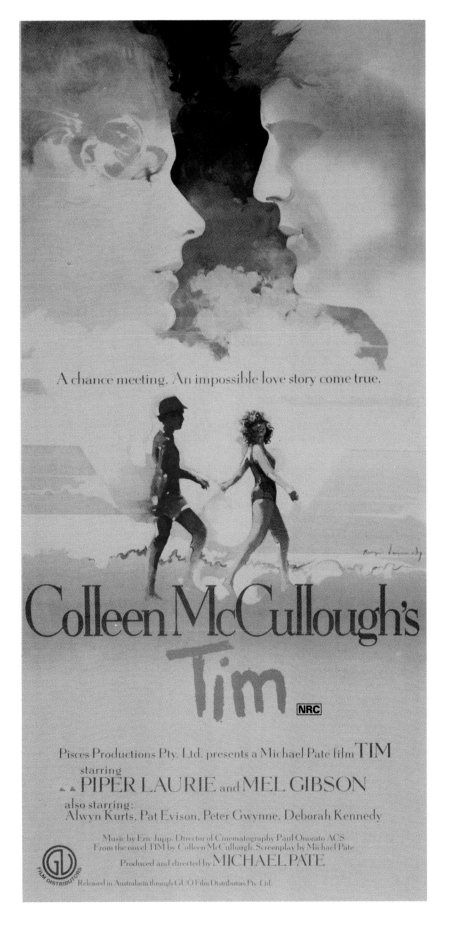

A chance meeting. An impossible love story come true.

Colleen McCullough's
Tim
NRC

Pisces Productions Pty. Ltd. presents a Michael Pate film TIM
starring
PIPER LAURIE and MEL GIBSON
also starring:
Alwyn Kurts, Pat Evison, Peter Gwynne, Deborah Kennedy
Music by Eric Jupp. Director of Cinematography Paul Onorato ACS
From the novel TIM by Colleen McCullough. Screenplay by Michael Pate
Produced and directed by MICHAEL PATE
Released in Australasia through GUO Film Distributors Pty. Ltd.

Gibson's performance in Tim *was not just an unexpectedly accomplished turn by a charismatic, rising new star but of a young actor who had solidly honed his craft.*

As she guides the simple but not stupid lad in reaching his full potential, Mary comes to emotionally depend on Tim as much as he does on her, and their relationship deepens. When Tim's mother dies and his father becomes too grief-stricken to care for the boy, Mary takes over the job full-time, with the father's blessing. But Tim's married sister Dawnie (Deborah Kennedy) is both jealous of Mary ("You're taking Tim from us") and outraged; she suspects Mary of lusting after her hunky but mentally handicapped brother.

Mary emphatically denies the accusation, but the way director Pate shoots some of the intimate scenes between Gibson's Tim and Piper Laurie's Mary, the viewer can't help but draw the same conclusion. For example, when Mary tucks Tim in bed one night, the romantic lighting of the scene, coupled with the not exactly subtle look of longing on the actress's face, clearly suggests that Mary might like to nuzzle up beside him. The scene makes the viewer feel a bit uneasy—reflecting, perhaps, Mary's own moral and emotional confusion— but it is not treated voyeuristically, with an eye toward titillation. *Tim* is a nice movie about decent and basically kindhearted people who only seek happiness for Tim and for themselves and hope they are doing the right thing. The film deals with its controversial subject matter somewhat superficially but not exploitatively.

In the same spirit, the film may be a tear-jerker, but it tries to move us honestly. Even the lump-in-the-throat scene between Dawnie and the now-married Tim at their father's funeral, where he begs her to love Mary as much as he does so they can be a family again, hints at the possibility of future reconciliation but doesn't say it's a certainty. As the film concludes, Mary and Tim and Dawnie and her husband walk away from the grave site at a distance from each other; they are still very much apart on the emotional issue which separates them—an ending that is wholly credible.

Tim is an actors' showcase, and the performances are uniformly excellent. Piper Laurie is somewhat indecipherable but ultimately touching as Mary, and Alwyn Kurts is superb as Tim's father. But the picture belongs to Mel Gibson; he is challenged to hold the whole thing together by bringing Tim alive and credibly sustaining the childlike wonderment that is the heart and soul of the character. And he rises to the task deftly.

Unlike many other actors, or actresses, who have had a go at playing mentally handicapped characters on-screen, he never lays it on thick by indulging in "watch me act" theatrics. In fact, he loses himself so convincingly in the part that he doesn't seem to *be* acting. His performance as Tim is not just an unexpectedly accomplished turn by a charismatic, rising new star, but of a young actor solidly in control of his craft.

ATTACK FORCE Z
(A.K.A. THE Z MEN)

1981—CENTRAL MOTION PICTURES CORPORATION

"I've done some really awful things, but Z-Men
is right at the top of the list."

—MEL GIBSON

CREDITS
Producer: Lee Robinson; *Director:* Tim Burstall; *Screenwriter:*
Roger Marshall; *Cinematographer:* Lin Hung-Chung; *Editor:*
David Stiven; *Composer:* Eric Jupp; *Production designer:*
Bernard Hides.
Running time: 84 minutes.

CAST
John Phillip Law *(Lt. Jan Veitch);* Mel Gibson *(Capt. Paul
Kelly);* Sam Neill *(Sgt. Danny Costello);* Chris Haywood
(Able Seaman Bird); John Waters *(Sublieutenant King);* Koo
Chuan-Hsiung *(Lin-Chan-Lang);* Sylvia Chang *(Chien
Hua);* O Ti *(Shaw tu);* Val Champion *(Ed Ayres).*

REVIEWS

*"As a good example of a well-paced, finely acted war
film, it is not much short of super. In fact, for success in achieving what its intention was, it is ahead
of many more vaunted Aussie productions."*

—VARIETY, 6/3/81

The title refers to an elite team of top-
secret commandos serving under Gen.
Douglas MacArthur in the South Pacific
during World War II. The Z Force was made up
of Australian, New Zealand, and other Allied
troops and was an actual World War II commando squad, according to an opening title
card. An association made up of surviving members of the actual Force Z (pronounced Zed)
served as technical advisers to bolster the scenario's authenticity, but the film emerges as just
an average action-adventure movie nonetheless.

The film takes place at the tail end of the
war in the Pacific in 1945. It focuses on an
impossible mission to rescue an important government official from a Japanese-held island in
the Sembalang Straits, where his American
plane was shot down. A five-man team from
Force Z is dropped off by submarine under
cover of night near the island, then proceeds
the rest of the way silently by canoe. In case one
of the team is captured by the Japanese and tortured for information during the course of the
mission, only squad leader Kelly (Mel Gibson)

The squad (Mel Gibson, John Waters, Sam Neill) links up with a member of the local resistance (Koo Chuan-Hsiung) to guide them in rescuing a high-level diplomat from a Japanese-held island.

has been told by his superiors a key secret: the VIP is a high-level Japanese defector on a peace mission that could foster a quick end to the war. Gibson is charged with bringing the man in or making sure he's dead, but at any and all costs not to allow the VIP to fall into the hands of his fellow Japanese.

It's Gibson's first time as squad leader, and he's a bit insecure about his decision-making abilities, often seeking from friend and subordinate Costello (Sam Neill) advice on, and approval of, his actions. But he's determined not to fail. "I didn't come here to lose," he tells his men, one of them, Veitch (Law), a relative

Now reduced to two, the Z men help the resistance fighters overthrow their Japanese oppressors.

of a Dutch planter on the island who was executed by the Japanese. Peace mission or not, the vengeful Veitch is all for shooting the VIP outright when he learns that the man is Japanese, too. But he's outvoted.

The squad links up with members of the local resistance, who guide them through the jungle to the downed plane and the VIP. Numerous firefights ensue along the way, resulting in a high body count of Japanese soldiers as well as exposure of the Z Force's presence on the island. The Japanese retaliate by taking civilians hostage and threatening to execute them

for helping the Allies. But the resistance and the Z Force show up in time to prevent too many atrocities and get the VIP to a waiting boat in the fiery finale—which concludes with a sardonic twist.

Gibson's role in *Attack Force Z* is a disappointing comedown from *Tim,* which gave him a choice opportunity to shine in the kind of part which, even then, the young actor felt was his metier: the romantic leading man with the shadings of a supporting character. As written, his squad leader, Captain Kelly, offered no similar challenge. It isn't a character part, nor is it the film's lead. That belongs to John Phillip Law's maverick Dutch commando, Lieutenant Veitch, who is not only given more screen time than Gibson in *Attack Force Z* but is the only character in the film to have a love interest—the daughter, Chien Hua, played by Sylvia Chang, of the island's resistance leader, Lin-Chan-Lang (Koo Chuan-Hsiung). A maverick to the end, Law eventually turns his back on the force (though not before dutifully seeing the mission through) by choosing to stay behind and help the resistance fighters overthrow their Japanese oppressors. Lead or not, the role is pretty thankless, as is the character's fate.

Gibson is suitably sturdy as the squad leader, but there is not much depth to his character or to any of his fellow squad members, either, including Law. He and his men never become individuals about whom we care, a major flaw, since the mission itself never quite engages us with a sense of urgency—probably because we're kept in the dark about it for at least half the film's length.

Screenwriter Roger Marshall's dialogue is a bit clunky as well, and the flow of events in his script is both disjointed and downright confusing at times. We're not always sure at a given moment who's doing what to whom or why. Most striking of all, the film's portrayal of the Japanese enemy is remarkably old-fashioned. Constantly threatening women and children with bullets and bayonets and tightening their lips in "yellow peril" menace, they seem more like characters from a propagandistic B war movie made long ago.

Still, there are a few suspenseful scenes in *Attack Force Z* and the action set pieces, especially the *Wild Bunch*–like finale, are well staged. There's even a little knife throwing and kung fu tossed in for good measure and diversity amid all the gunfire. And the scene in which Sam Neill shoots a wounded comrade when the squad realizes it can neither take the man along nor leave him behind to be captured is both unexpected and shocking due to the sudden and chillingly offhand manner in which it is treated.

Commandos Gibson, Waters, and Neill.

GALLIPOLI

1981—PARAMOUNT

"I felt myself completely involved in it. I can do that when I get a truthful subject or truthful relationships to work with—and this film had both."

—MEL GIBSON

CREDITS

Producers: Robert Stigwood and Patricia Lovell; *Director:* Peter Weir; *Screenwriter:* David Williamson, based on a story by Peter Weir; *Cinematographer:* Russell Boyd; *Editor:* William Anderson; *Composer:* Brian May; *Production designer:* Wendy Weir.
Running time: 110 minutes.

CAST

Mark Lee *(Archy);* Bill Kerr *(Jack);* Mel Gibson *(Frank Dunne);* Ronnie Graham *(Wallace Hamilton);* Harold Hopkins *(Les McCann);* Charles Yunupingu *(Zac);* Heath Harris *(Stockman);* Gerda Nicolson *(Rose Hamilton);* Robert Grubb *(Billy);* Tim McKenzie *(Barney);* David Argue *(Snowy);* Reg Evans *(Official 1);* Jack Giddy *(Official 2);* Dane Peterson *(Announcer);* Paul Linkson *(Recruiting Officer).*

Frank races through the trenches to deliver the order calling a halt to the suicidal charge that will soon claim the life of his friend.

REVIEWS

"It's hard to think of any recent performances in American films as direct and joyful as those of Mark Lee and Mel Gibson, both of whom exude an unabashed masculinity reminiscent of Old Hollywood. The lack of both swagger and neurosis is extremely appealing."

—WOMEN'S WEAR DAILY, 8/24/81

"Gallipoli is an absorbing film and a moving lament for a brave and betrayed generation."

—NEWSWEEK, 9/7/81

"Well acted and, within its limited terms, well made, Gallipoli represents a failure of nerve as well as design."

—TIME, 9/14/81

"The acting is quite superb. Mel Gibson is charming and ultimately touching as the swaggering Frank."

—FILMS IN REVIEW, 10/81

Archy and Frank are given a hero's sendoff on their way to the front.

Unlike *Attack Force Z*, Peter Weir's *Gallipoli* is not a war movie so much as a film of symbol, metaphor, and irony set against the backdrop of war. It bridges the director's early, cerebral thrillers (*Picnic at Hanging Rock* [1975], *The Last Wave* [1977]) and the more emotional human dramas (*Witness* [1985], *Fearless* [1993]) he would make in the years ahead. As a result, Weir's approach to his material is still somewhat distanced as well as distancing; thus, the film, while impeccably made and acted, winds up being more of a moving lament to the defining moment in Australia's history it portrays than the devastating grand tragedy it strives to be.

The film's major symbol is Gallipoli itself, a strip of coastline in the Dardanelles that served as the Allies' embattled front line of defense against the Turks during World War I; in constant need of reinforcements to stem the enemy tide, the area became a magnet which drew thousands of young Australians to enlist for God and country.

Two of these young men are Archy and Frank. Both are championship runners, but each represents a different side of the Australian character.

Archy (Mark Lee) is the more dreamy-eyed and idealistic of the pair. He views enlisting as his patriotic duty; continuing the racing metaphor which runs throughout the film, he's the type who always goes the distance—for family, friends, or country. In fact, he puts on hold his burgeoning athletic career and dreams of becoming the next Australian world-champion runner to join the cause.

On the other hand, Frank (Mel Gibson) is more pragmatic, even cynical, the more cocksure and stereotypically Aussie of the duo. He enlists because he's sick of drifting aimlessly through life and being broke much of the time. He plans to keep his head down, learn a trick or two, and "come back a bloody officer" so he won't have to get shoved around for the rest of his life. Patriotism doesn't enter into it for him. "It's not our bloody war," he counsels Archy. "It's an English war."

However, both young men are lured to

Both men wind up serving in the trenches of Gallipoli, where wave upon wave of Australians are mowed down in a diversionary action against the Turks.

their rendezvous with fate at Gallipoli by their mutual thirst for adventure and desire for action.

They meet at a track competition where Frank loses the race to Archy by a nose, even though Archy isn't in top form: His feet are still lacerated and bleeding from an impetuous wager made on the eve of the track meet that he could outrun a taunting friend on horseback in his bare feet.

They become mates. Frank, a city boy from Perth with street smarts, helps the underage Archy pull a fast one to get by the age requirements for enlistment. They hop a train to Perth, where Archy isn't known, and Frank forges some credentials for him. Later, Archy, a cattleman's son from the Australian outback, gives Frank some pointers on horsemanship so that Frank can escape being assigned to the lowly, dreaded infantry and get into the more glamorous Lighthorse Cavalry Division to which Archy has been assigned. Nevertheless, Frank's inexperience on horseback quickly reveals itself; he is rejected by the Lighthorse, and the two

Lured to their rendezvous with fate by a thirst for adventure and desire for action: the betrayed young men of Gallipoli.

friends are separated.

Ironically, Frank winds up serving in the infantry he'd sought to avoid. More ironically yet, both men wind up serving alongside each other in the trenches of Gallipoli, where the Australians are caught up in a deadly diversionary action against the Turks to prevent landing British reinforcements from being slaughtered.

Wave upon wave of Australians are cut down in repeated assaults against the Turks. Ultimately, Archy's fate and that of hundreds of others charged with mounting a final assault on the enemy's guns depends on Frank's ability as a runner to be faster on his feet for once than Archy. When it is learned that the British troops have successfully landed, he must get back to the trenches in time with an order to call a halt to the assault.

Archy and Frank's commanding officer, Major Barton (Bill Hunter), who had seen Archy beat Frank in the track meet early on in the film, seeks out Archy for the vital job of communications runner ("A few extra seconds can save a lot of lives"), but Archy is determined to get into the fray. Without Frank's knowledge, Archy recommends Frank for the assignment to keep his friend out of harm's way, and the commander reluctantly agrees. The bitter irony is that Archy, the superior runner, might have made it. But despite a Herculean effort, Frank again proves second best, arriving just as the

command is given to send Archy and the others over the top to sure death. Frank cries out in anguish at being too late. The final image is a freeze frame of Archy caught at the moment of death as the Turkish machine-gun fire slams into his chest.

The image burns in the memory, but overall the film lacks the power of such earlier movies on a similar theme as Lewis Milestone's *All Quiet on the Western Front* (1930), a film that also concludes with a potent close-up of one of its betrayed and wasted young heroes at the moment of death.

Gallipoli engages our senses with its meticulous re-creation of period, breathtaking landscapes and striking images of men at war—the landing of Archy, Frank, and their comrades on the shores of Gallipoli in small boats during a nighttime bombardment is especially stunning. And the film succeeds to a degree in stirring our outrage at the utter waste of it all by making us feel something for Archy and Frank, largely due to the performances of Mark Lee and Mel Gibson, who bring considerable charm to their costarring roles, even though the characters themselves never quite rise above type. But overall *Gallipoli* is more an epic of scope and theme than of heart, and as a tribute to Australia's fallen sons at Gallipoli, it tends to haunt the mind rather than overwhelm the emotions.

MAD MAX 2: THE ROAD WARRIOR

1981—WARNER BROS.

"I like watching that film. It's a total freakout."

—MEL GIBSON

CREDITS

Producer: Byron Kennedy; *Director:* George Miller; *Screenwriters:* Terry Hayes, George Miller, and Brian Hannant; *Cinematographer:* Dean Semler; *Editors:* David Stiven, Tim Wellburn, and Michael Chirgwin; *Composer:* Brian May; *Art director:* Graham Walker. Running time: 94 minutes.

CAST

Mel Gibson *(Max);* Bruce Spence *(Gyro Captain);* Vernon Wells *(Wez);* Emil Minty *(Feral Kid);* Mike Preston *(Pappagallo);* Kjell Nilsson *(Humungus);* Virginia Hey *(Warrior Woman);* Syd Heylen *(Curmudgeon);* Moira Claux *(Big Rebecca);* David Slingsby *(Quiet Man);* Arkie Whiteley *(Lusty Girl);* Steve J. Spears *(Mechanic);* Max Phipps *(Toadie);* William Zappa *(Farmer);* Jimmy Brown *(Golden Youth).*

REVIEWS

"Mad Max 2 is a stunning technical achievement which far surpasses the first Max film in every department. The title character is still a man of few words, but fleshed out better by Gibson, who proved his worth in Gallipoli."

—VARIETY, 12/23/81

"When our anti-hero appeared in Mad Max, he was an amoral vigilante with baby fat. Since then, Gallipoli has made Gibson an international star: he is more mature and authoritative; his moon face is cratered with character."

—TIME, 5/10/82

"Much of its success depends on the strength of Mel Gibson, who plays the title character. Gibson has a sangfroid, an unself-conscious steeliness that sets him apart from most contemporary leading men. He has none of the currently fashionable vulnerability that is supposed to make men of action more sympathetic; instead there is a sense of determination and conviction about him that recalls Hollywood heroes of another era."

—WOMEN'S WEAR DAILY, 8/18/82

"Mel Gibson who has been in better pictures, notably Tim and Gallipoli, is a good-looking lad. The film should give hyperactive kids with no critical faculties a good workout."

—NEW YORK POST, 8/20/82

No longer an avenger, Max is merely trying to get by as best he can in a violent and amoral world.

"My life fades, the vision dims. All that remains are memories . . ." laments the narrator in the opening sequence of the film, a somber but relentlessly action filled follow-up to the original *Mad Max,* set in the warrior wastelands of Australia a few years hence. In many respects, *Mad Max 2: The Road Warrior* is also a reworking of the classic George Stevens western *Shane* (1953).

Over a backdrop of stark black-and-white images, the narrator recounts the events that threw the world into chaos before the first *Mad Max* began, sketching in many of the sociopo-

A man alone, a tragic hero who cannot escape his past, his only companion a dog to which he hasn't given a name.

litical details the original hadn't provided. We think the narrator is Max himself. But when the film reaches its conclusion, we realize this is not the case when the narrator mournfully says, "As for the road warrior [Max], it was the last we ever saw of him. He lives only in my memories."

The narrator is actually the Feral Kid (played by Emil Minty), a wild child of the postapocalypse who falls under the spell of the oil-scavenging road-warrior Max in much the same way—and for many of the same reasons— that Brandon De Wilde's frontier child falls under the spell of Alan Ladd's gunfighter in *Shane.* He learns much from Max, whose influence enables the boy to grow up and assume leadership of his wasteland tribe. But Max is, like Shane, a man alone, a tragic hero who cannot

graying at the temples. His only companion is a dog, which, perhaps to avoid the pitfalls of attachment, Max hasn't even given a name. He just calls it "Dog."

Max subsists on cans of dog food, taking his fill first, then giving the scraps to the animal. He traverses the landscape in his battered but still souped-up V-8 with but two purposes: finding the next precious drop of gasoline that will take him from one aimless destination to the next and staying alive in the process.

No longer an avenger, Max is simply trying to get by as best he can in a violent and amoral universe, like the existential heroes of classic films noir of the 1940s whose mood *Mad Max 2: The Road Warrior* successfully emulates.

escape the past, which prevents him from being a leader himself. In *Mad Max 2: The Road Warrior,* he is the man who fosters leadership in others, the man who paves the way for them to achieve what he himself cannot. The film marks the first major appearance of this ongoing theme, in the many films of Mel Gibson as actor and/or director, which would reach its most passionate expression in *Braveheart.*

The film resumes Max's saga a few years after the first film ends. His leather outfit is no longer as shiny black as it was, but well worn and caked with wasteland dust—much like Max himself, who has aged dramatically in appearance, if not in actual years.

By now, Gibson's Max has become the full-blown character part not possible in the first film because the character wasn't as seasoned yet. His face is fuller now, and grizzled, his hair

Max's loner status makes him a perfect target for predators bent on stealing his V-8's gasoline. As a result, he has booby-trapped the car to explode should anyone try to siphon gas from the fuel tank.

From an encounter with another wanderer, the Gyro Captain (portrayed by Bruce Spence), who uses a poisonous snake to protect the precious fuel in his airborne vehicle, Max learns of a rumored fuel reserve located somewhere in the desert.

The two team up and find it—a tanker that has been walled in like a fortress by an outnumbered group using flamethrowers to ward off the constant attacks of outlaw bikers trying to get their hands on the hoarded gas inside.

Max prevents the bikers from breaking through but accepts no thanks from the fortress's defenders for his heroics. "Save it," he

Preferring to do his own stunts for the film, Gibson got fairly bruised and banged up in the making of Mad Max 2: The Road Warrior. *Director George Miller is at left.*

snaps at the group's leader. "I'm here for the gasoline." In exchange for that gasoline, he agrees to help the group find a truck capable of hauling the tanker to a new location—a sort of promised land known by the group only through an old and well-thumbed tourism brochure. Max is skeptical of the group's plan, having no belief in a promised land himself, but fulfills his bargain and gets the truck, increasing the wrath of the bikers, who vow to get him.

Asked to drive the truck when the fortress's defenders make their break, Max declines. He takes his gasoline and leaves. Chased by the bikers, he is almost killed, and his V-8 is destroyed. Looking like a wraith from hell, he returns to the fortress. His V-8 gone for good, he insists on driving the truck, his only way out.

This leads to the film's exciting denouement, a lengthy, spectacularly choreographed and edited race along the desert highway as Max tries to outrun and outflank the murderous bikers, who descend on the tanker like flies, paying no attention to the fortress's defenders who are getting away.

The pulse-pounding sequence culminates in a marvelous twist that I won't reveal except to say that it leaves Max standing, shows that even the wiliest of heroes can be cunningly manipulated, and nicely summarizes the film's theme.

THE YEAR OF LIVING DANGEROUSLY

1983—METRO-GOLDWYN-MAYER

"Dimensionwise, [the character of] Guy Hamilton provided a very limited framework for an actor. He really was just a puppet, though not such a dud as he was in the book."

—MEL GIBSON

CREDITS

Producer: James McElroy; *Director:* Peter Weir; *Screenwriters:* David Williamson, Peter Weir, and C. J. Koch, based on the novel by Koch; *Cinematographer:* Russell Boyd; *Editor:* Bill Anderson; *Composer:* Maurice Jarre; *Art director:* Herbert Pinter.
Running time: 115 minutes.

CAST

Mel Gibson *(Guy Hamilton);* Sigourney Weaver *(Jill Bryant);* Linda Hunt *(Billy Kwan);* Michael Murphy *(Pete Curtis);* Bembol Roco *(Kumar);* Domingo Landicho *(Hortono);* Hermono De Guzman *(Immigration Officer);* Noel Ferrier *(Wally O'Sullivan);* Paul Sonkkila *(Kevin Condon);* Ali Nur *(Ali);* Dominador Robridillo *(Betjak Man);* Joel Agona *(Palace Guard);* Mike Emperio *(President Sukarno);* Bernardo Nacilla *(Dwarf);* Bill Kerr *(Colonel Henderson).*

REVIEWS

"Gibson, the U.S. born Australian star of Gallipoli *and* The Road Warrior, *brings a cocky Yank vulnerability to his role."*

—TIME, 1/17/83

"If this film doesn't make an international star of Mr. Gibson, then nothing will. He possesses both the necessary talent and the screen presence."

—NEW YORK TIMES, 1/21/83

"Mel Gibson, the handsome American-born Australian dreamboat, seems to be suffering from either malnutrition or malaria."

—NEW YORK POST, 1/21/83

"Mel Gibson, looking slimmer without his road-warrior armor, sets his virile jaw and then smiles engagingly as Guy Hamilton, a young, untested Australian radio-TV journalist assigned to Jakarta."

—NEW YORK, 1/24/83

"Gibson . . . seems determined not to find the shadings that his role needs if this story is going to make sense. (The young William Holden could have done wonders with the part.)

—NEWSWEEK, 1/24/83

As Guy Hamilton in The Year of Living Dangerously. *"If this film doesn't make an international star out of Mr. Gibson, then nothing will," wrote Vincent Canby in the* New York Times.

Weaver and Gibson spark chemistry together as the lovers who have skirted roadblocks and outrun shooting guards to find the nearest bed.

Like the character he played in Peter Weir's *Gallipoli*, Gibson's character in the same director's *The Year of Living Dangerously* also journeys to a far-off land for an appointment with destiny that forces him to grow up and mature.

A novice correspondent for the Australia Broadcasting Service (ABS), Gibson's Guy Hamilton is sent to Dakarta, where President Sukarno is walking a precarious tightrope between the Communists on the Left and the military extremists on the Right. Hamilton views the assignment as little more than a stepping-stone to Vietnam, a country, already embroiled in civil war, where the real journalistic action is. All he needs is one big scoop to get him there. Unfortunately, he has been dumped into his first assignment in Djakarta without any contacts. He quickly finds himself professionally adrift. Competing with the more experienced reporters covering the same beat for other media who do have contacts, he is scooped time and time again.

This changes when Hamilton meets an inscrutable little Indonesian named Billy Kwan, who takes the reporter under his wing. A freelance photographer of Chinese-Australian extraction, the dwarfish Billy is a staunch Sukarno supporter; he views the president in almost mystical terms, as the Godlike savior of his people. In the wide-eyed, ambitious, but unseasoned and uncynical Hamilton, Billy sees just the man to get the real story of his impoverished homeland—the truth behind the headlines—out to the world. They make a deal. Billy uses his numerous contacts to get Hamilton an exclusive interview with the leader of the country's Communist Party; in exchange, Hamilton gives Billy all the photographic work the little man can handle. The two become inseparable.

Hamilton arouses his colleagues' jealousy with his first scoop that the Communists are pushing Sukarno to sever all ties to the West and that their strength is gaining. When an even bigger story comes his way—that the Communists are receiving arms shipments to mount an insurrection—Hamilton zealously reports it, regardless of the danger it places his contacts in; many of them wind up on death lists. This turns the idealistic Billy against Hamilton; he accuses the reporter of being morally adrift, a self-serving, scoop-hungry journalist, just like all the rest.

When the military seizes control of the government to defeat the Communists, Sukarno (Mike Emperio) reveals himself to be just another self-serving politician; he goes along and becomes a puppet to maintain his lavish lifestyle. The despondent Billy turns against his former God and is killed after committing an act of political protest.

As the military cracks down, the country is thrown into civil war. On his own, Hamilton seeks a final scoop, an exclusive interview with the right-wing military leaders, and almost loses his life. He escapes the country by the skin of his teeth, hopping aboard the last plane out, a

A novice correspondent for the Australian Broadcasting Service, Hamilton is sent to cover the pending civil war in Dakarta.

sadder but wiser and better man now as a result of the eye-opening year of living dangerously— the same span of time the equally self-serving but ultimately corrupt Sukarno spent perform- ing his delicate balancing act.

A love affair between Gibson's Hamilton and Sigourney Weaver's Jill Bryant, an assistant to the British military attaché in Dakarta, mixes with the turmoil and mirrors the larger political events of the film. It is Billy Kwan who introduces Hamilton to Jill. In love with Jill himself but incapable of having her, Billy makes Hamilton his surrogate and manipulates their affair.

But the personal story is never quite as involving as the political one it parallels. Except for the scene in which Gibson and Weaver cut loose from an embassy party after curfew and rouse themselves to a sexual pitch skirting roadblocks and outrunning shooting guards to find the nearest bed, their affair lacks passion—certainly the grand passion of other classic movie romances set against a political backdrop, such as *Casablanca* (1942) and *Notorious* (1946), which *The Year of Living Dangerously* calls to mind. However, Gibson and Weaver do spark chemistry together, especially in the above-mentioned scene.

It's never really clear why Hamilton is so hooked on Jill apart from the fact that he's a bachelor, she's the prettiest and most desirable girl around, and Billy *wants* the two of them to fall in love. There isn't much substance to the

Linda Hunt as Billy Kwan, the inscrutable freelance photographer of Chinese-Australian extraction who takes the unseasoned Hamilton under his wing.

88

Hamilton sets out to get the truth behind the headlines, placing himself in constant danger.

woman's character. But the same can be said of Hamilton himself. He engages us largely due to Gibson's inherent likability on the screen and that oft overused word "charisma," in the role. The actor admits to having considerable difficulty putting flesh on the rather one-dimensional character's bones.

In fact, the most fascinating character in the film (as in the novel, from which the film was derived) is Billy Kwan. In an offbeat bit of casting which the coscreenwriter and author of the novel, C. J. Koch, adamantly opposed, the role was given to the diminutive American actress Linda Hunt, who won a Best Supporting Actress Oscar for her performance.

She and the vivid third world atmosphere Weir poetically evokes in *The Year of Living Dangerously* are what bring the film to life and linger in the memory.

THE BOUNTY

1984—ORION

8

"The character [of Fletcher Christian] was lacking, and the only place [I could do] something was in the mutiny scene when he flips out."

—MEL GIBSON

CREDITS

Producer: Bernard Williams; *Director:* Roger Donaldson; *Screenwriter:* Robert Bolt, based on the book *Captain Bligh and Mr. Christian* by Richard Hough; *Cinematographer:* Arthur Ibbetson; *Editor:* Tony Lawson; *Composer:* Vangelis; *Production designer:* John Graysmark.
Running time: 130 minutes.

CAST

Mel Gibson *(Fletcher Christian);* Anthony Hopkins *(Lt. William Bligh);* Laurence Olivier *(Admiral Hood);* Edward Fox *(Captain Greetham);* Daniel Day Lewis *(Fryer);* Bernard Hill *(Cole);* Philip Davis *(Young);* Liam Neeson *(Churchill);* Wi Kuki Kaa *(King Tynah);* Tevaite Vernette *(Mauatua);* Philip Martin Brown *(Adams);* Simon Chandler *(Nelson);* Malcolm Terris *(Dr. Huggan);* Simon Adams *(Heywood);* John Sessions *(Smith).*

REVIEWS

"Gibson, thick eyelashes notwithstanding, is the film's weak link. At first it seems hardly his fault, since he is given little to do but be peripheral to the action. But his peak scene, as he must wrestle in anguish between duty and the preservation of the crew, is a dramatic embarrassment."

—LOS ANGELES TIMES, 5/4/84

"Mel Gibson's Fletcher Christian is little more than a fun-loving party guy who 'goes native' in Tahiti and resents being forced to return to England."

—NEWSDAY, 5/4/84

"Gibson cuts a dashing and romantic figure, but much of the time he has nothing to do but look sullen and confused."

—NEWSWEEK, 5/14/94

"Mel Gibson's [Fletcher] Christian has been written largely as a petulantly inarticulate rock star with more charisma than conversation."

—VILLAGE VOICE, 5/15/84

Though Christian fails as a leader himself, his mutiny fosters greater leadership in Bligh, a recurring theme in the films of Mel Gibson.

uthors Charles Nordhoff and James Norman Hall required three novels to tell their version of the *Mutiny on the Bounty* and its aftermath, although only the first volume of their trilogy (the other two were *Men Against the Sea* and *Pitcairn Island*) was filmed—twice. Therefore, it was not unreasonable for director David Lean, at the outset, to feel he needed to make two films to tell the same story when he embarked on his ill-fated epic version of the saga drawn from Richard Hough's revisionist history *Captain Bligh and Mr. Christian*. As a result, the single film, cobbled together from Robert Bolt's two screenplays for Lean, which finally reached the screen in 1984 as *The Bounty*—minus Lean's involvement—has a distinctly truncated feel to it.

Important secondary characters reveal tantalizing glimpses of the greater significance they may have had in the motives behind the mutiny and its tragic aftermath in Bolt's longer individual scripts but wind up as little more than caricatures or types in the combined screenplay here. And the compelling story of Bligh's survival at sea with his men after being jettisoned from the *Bounty* as well as the hunt for and fate of the mutineers afterward is pared down to a few brief sequences. What we are left with is a retelling of the familiar story of the mutiny itself, and while given a more truthful new twist, it seems much less dynamic and smaller in scale

Lieutenant Bligh (Anthony Hopkins, seated left), Christian (Mel Gibson), and the crew of the Bounty *arrive in the island paradise of Tahiti.*

92

than its two previous, albeit fictionalized, screen treatments.

That being said, *The Bounty* is by no means the complete failure its critical reputation would suggest. No, the film isn't as exciting as the 1935 *Mutiny on the Bounty* with Clark Gable or as "big" as the 1962 *Mutiny* with Marlon Brando. And yes, it has a "We've seen it all before" quality. But there's more here than meets the eye, especially in Mel Gibson's misjudged and unfairly dismissed performance as Fletcher Christian, a character he manages to turn very much into his own despite being given little to work with in the watered-down script.

The film begins with a military inquiry into the mutiny and its wake, which Bligh explains in a series of flashbacks, beginning with his friendship with Christian, a young but experienced seaman Bligh persuades to be his master's mate because he needs a man he feels he can trust.

The ambitious Bligh sees in the voyage to Tahiti for breadfruit plants a golden opportunity to make a name for himself in His Majesty's service. He determines to set a round-trip record by taking the *Bounty* around Cape Horn in the dead of winter to make up time. But a crew member is killed, and the ship almost capsizes in the stormy weather, setting the *Bounty*, which now is forced to turn back and take the longer route, months behind schedule. Bligh owns up to this mistake but places the blame for his future miscalculations and misjudgments on others, including, increasingly, Christian himself.

Christian (Mel Gibson) falls in love with the chief's daughter, Mauatua, played by Tevaite Vernette.

As Fletcher Christian, a high-seas "rebel without a cause."

The film hints that the older Bligh may have had a homosexual crush on the handsome, twenty-two-year-old Christian—an almost obligatory subtext in most movies these days dealing with any relationship between two men—and that he cracked up emotionally after seeing Christian carrying on with a gorgeous native girl in the heterosexual paradise of Tahiti, thus setting the wheels in motion for the mutiny. But the real nature of their relationship, at least the one the film expresses most clearly, is that of stern, overdemanding father and wayward, recalcitrant son.

Unlike other screen Blighs, Anthony Hopkins's Bligh is a rigid, though not unduly harsh, disciplinarian. He merely keeps a tight ship. However, over the course of the voyage to Tahiti, he becomes increasingly disenchanted with the well-connected Christian for lacking in drive and ambition and for not living up to the expectations he has of the young man; he starts cracking down on the crew to give the youth an object lesson in leadership, a lesson Christian resists.

The contest of wills comes to a head in Tahiti, where Christian falls in love with the

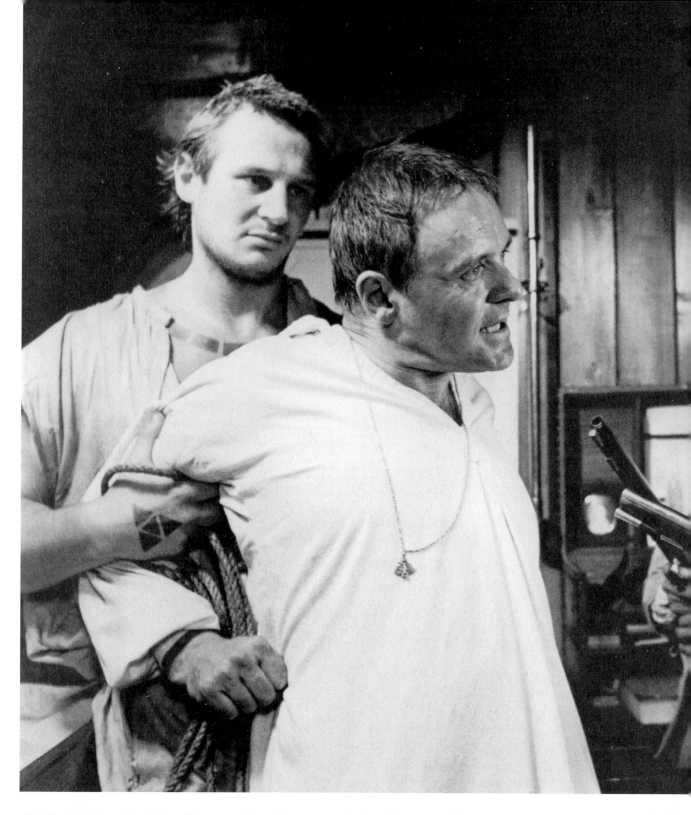

chief's daughter, has himself tattooed, and goes native like a lowly deckhand. "You needed someone to tell you where your duty really lay. You were at a loss, my friend," Bligh tells the lad, cutting the sojourn in Tahiti short. But Christian responds sullenly, his reaction to being told what's best for him resembling that of a headstrong adolescent to a lecture from an unreasonable dad he sees as being totally out of it. Furious, Bligh comes down hard, becoming, in Christian's eyes, the "parent from hell."

Feeling they wasted too much time in Tahiti and blaming Christian for it, Bligh decides to make a second stab at rounding the

Bligh takes Christian's warnings of mutiny as a personal threat. Angry, Christian responds by leading it—the ultimate act of adolescent rebellion against parental authority. Also pictured: Liam Neeson, Philip Davis, and Dennis Fletcher.

self. Angry, Christian responds by leading it.

Mel Gibson was scorned by many critics for coming across like a hysterical child in the scene in which he seizes the ship. In fact, that very scene is what the actor's performance has been leading up to all along, and Gibson brings it off superbly; it's the most electrifying moment in the movie because it's what the mutiny in *The Bounty*, a seagoing *Rebel Without a Cause*, is all about—the ultimate act of adolescent rebellion against parental authority.

As their contest of wills reaches critical mass, Christian screams, "I am in hell," at Bligh, his astonished and uncomprehending father figure, echoing James Dean's cry "Stop, you're tearing me apart" in that earlier film about the pains and perils of growing up, not to mention the cries of the anguished young prince of Denmark in *Hamlet*.

Ironically, while the impetuous mutiny results in personal tragedy for Christian, who subsequently fails as a leader himself, it fosters greater leadership in Bligh. His heroic voyage across six-hundred miles of ocean in an open launch to save those loyal to him results in Bligh's exoneration on all charges of inciting the mutiny with his methods and earns him the name and promotion he wanted but might not have achieved if it weren't for Fletcher Christian.

Horn to shorten the voyage back. Fearing for their lives, the crew threatens mutiny. Dutifully, Christian warns Bligh of this, but "father and son" are now at such loggerheads in their battle of wills that communication between them is no longer possible. Bligh takes the warning of mutiny as a personal threat from Christian him-

MRS. SOFFEL

1984—METRO-GOLDWYN-MAYER

"What appealed to me [in the script] was the [prison] bars. It's interesting how [the two characters] work to get around them, and eventually they lose them. There's always a good obstacle in a good love story."

—MEL GIBSON

CREDITS

Producers: Scott Rudin, Edgar J. Scherick, and David Nicksay; *Director:* Gillian Armstrong; *Screenwriter:* Ron Nyswaner; *Cinematographer:* Russell Boyd; *Editor:* Nicholas Beauman; *Composer:* Mark Isham; *Production designers:* Liciana Arrighi and Roy Forge Smith.
Running time: 113 minutes.

CAST

Mel Gibson *(Eddie Biddle);*
Diane Keaton *(Kate Soffel);* Edward Herrmann *(Peter Soffel);* Matthew Modine *(Jack Biddle);* Terry O'Quinn *(Buck McGovern);* Daniel Bryan Corkill *(Eddie Soffel);* Trini Alvarado *(Irene Soffel);* Harley Cross *(Clarence Soffel);* Jennie Dundas *(Margaret Soffel);* Frank Adamson *(Swinehart);* Rodger Barton *(Deputy Hoon);* James Bradford *(Minister);* Valerie Buhagiar *(Alice);* Alar Aedma *(Guard);* John Carroll *(Guard McGarey);* Maurey Chakin *(Guard Reynolds).*

REVIEWS

"Gibson . . . has mastered a slight midwestern drawl that evokes both Henry Fonda and John Wayne. Like those two supremely confident actors, he merely offers his words, without any special pressure, just letting them float in the air. Take it or leave it. And what woman in her right mind would leave it?"

—NEW YORK, 1/14/85

"Mel Gibson gets to show more range than he ever has; though there is still something a little bland and generalized about his acting, he makes his sharpest impression here."

—NEWSWEEK, 1/14/85

Mrs. *Soffel* is a somber romance loosely based on a forgotten incident in the folklore of American crime: The wife of a prison warden falls for a condemned prisoner, helps him escape, joins him in his failed flight, and winds up in the slammer herself, her

When Mrs. Soffel (Diane Keaton) helps Eddie break out, his refusal to leave without her makes her realize he's in love with her after all. The two become wanted fugitives.

Mrs. Soffel (Diane Keaton), the wife of the prison warden, falls for the condemned prisoner (Mel Gibson), who has aroused her passion, fully aware that he is manipulating her into helping him escape.

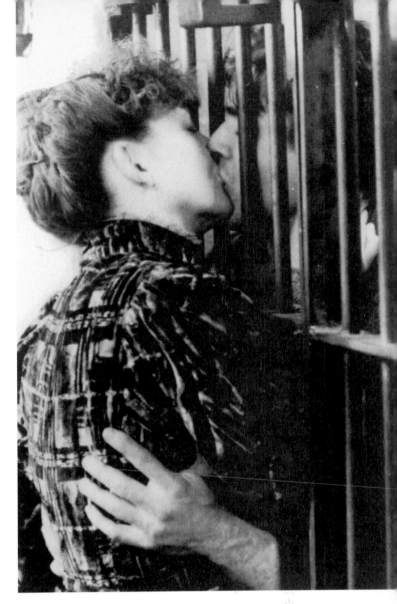

name and reputation destroyed for the sake of love.

The scandalous 1902 case made headlines across the country and inspired a stage melodrama that continued playing to packed houses well into the 1920s, when the woman (whose actual name was Scoffel) died in anonymity at age forty.

The movie portrays Kate Soffel (Diane Keaton) as an unfulfilled woman locked in a passionless marriage to a stern, unhandsome man she can no longer bear to sleep with. When not totally incapacitated due to chronic malaise, she distributes Bibles to the prison inmates, urging them to find solace in religion, just as she has done. She falls under the spell of Eddie Biddle (Gibson), the older of two brothers who have landed on death row for the murder of a grocer during an armed robbery.

The boys claim to be innocent scapegoats railroaded by the testimony of a third partner who got off scot-free for turning state's evidence. Eddie insists it was this third partner who actually committed the murder. Their case has aroused the interest of anti-death-penalty advocates and suffragettes as well as the passions of lovesick young girls turned on by Eddie's matinee-idol looks and swashbuckling reputation.

Fairly soon, Mrs. Soffel finds herself as attracted to Eddie as the giddy young girls parading outside the prison walls hoping for a glimpse of him. As she reads passages from the Bible to Eddie through the bars of his cell, he reads her like a book; he plays on her repressed longing to break free of her own prison to foster an identification with his plight and lay the groundwork for an escape.

By resisting her overtures of compassion at first ("You don't know what it's like to be in here," he snaps through the bars), then slowly coming around and wooing her with notes pro-

Back in his cell, Eddie continues to write Mrs. Soffel love notes until he is hanged. The real Eddie was killed in a gun battle with police.

fessing love and redemption, he skillfully plays on her pent-up passion and manipulates their platonic friendship into a clandestine affair. She's fully aware of his manipulations but doesn't care if he's lying about being in love with her. The relationship makes her feel alive.

When the governor refuses to commute the boys' sentence and the execution is scheduled, Eddie asks her to slip him some hacksaw blades and a gun. She does, and the boys break out. Eddie comes for her in her room; he insists he won't leave without her, and she realizes he's in love with her, after all. The three become wanted fugitives.

Eddie and Mrs. Soffel eventually consummate their love affair in a farmer's home shortly before being tracked down by police. Caught in an ambush like Bonnie and Clyde, she begs Eddie to shoot her so she can die in his arms.

Mrs. Soffel, Eddie, and Eddie's brother Jack (Matthew Modine) fight the elements seeking freedom in Canada.

He does. Eddie's brother Jack (Matthew Modine) is killed in the ambush, and Eddie is wounded and recaptured. Mrs. Soffel survives the gunshot and is sentenced to a stretch in the ladies' wing of the same prison where she once distributed Bibles. From his cell in the men's wing, Eddie continues to write love notes to her until he is hanged.

In fact, the real Eddie Biddle was killed, along with his brother, in the gun battle with police. He was also guilty of the murder that landed him in prison—an issue this romanticized version of the tale doesn't exactly skirt but treats with kid gloves.

In the scene in which Eddie finally comes clean with his lover about his guilt or innocence, the script has him do so in veiled terms so that his character and hers don't lose our sympathy. The real story had a harder and more disagreeable edge, for Mrs. Scoffel did know Eddie was guilty; she just didn't care.

Mrs. Soffel is strong in atmosphere and per- formance but rather emotionless as a love story. The romance between the two characters remains strangely subdued even after the prison break and the two can finally indulge their passion. Their spirits lift from being together at last, but the buoyant mood of these scenes is tempered by the harsh winter landscapes in which the characters are trapped while taking flight—beautifully photographed though these landscapes are by cameraman Russell Boyd.

Mrs. Soffel is portrayed as a heroine, but if the film is intended as a feminist message that women should follow their hearts regardless of the consequences, that message seems dubious as well as irresponsible, given its framework here, for Mrs. Soffel turns her back on her family, which includes several small children, to run off with Eddie. If the genders were reversed and Warden Soffel abandoned his children to run off with a female prisoner, feminists would surely want to see the bastard strung up. And rightly so.

THE RIVER

1984—UNIVERSAL

"I think I did a real bad job. I was young and stupid. And I was trying to phone [my performance] in."

—MEL GIBSON

CREDITS

Producers: Edward Lewis and Robert Cortes; *Director:* Mark Rydell; *Screenwriters:* Robert Dillon and Julian Barry; *Cinematographer:* Vilmos Zsigmond; *Editor:* Sidney Levin; *Composer:* John Williams; *Production designer:* Charles Rosen.
Running time: 122 minutes.

CAST

Mel Gibson *(Tom Garvey);* Sissy Spacek *(Mae Garvey);* Shane Bailey *(Lewis Garvey);* Becky Jo Lynch *(Beth Garvey);* Scott Glenn *(Joe Wade);* Don Hood *(Senator Neiswinder);* Billy "Green" Bush *(Harve Stanley);* James Tolkan *(Howard Simpson);* Bob W. Douglas *(Hal Richardson);* Andy Stahl *(Dave Birkin);* Lisa Sloan *(Judy Birkin);* Larry D. Ferrell *(Rod Tessley);* Susie Toomey *(Sally Tessley);* Kelly Toomey *(Lisa Tessley);* Frank Taylor *(Zemke).*

REVIEWS

"Mel Gibson, the American-born Australian heart-throb, proves he's not just another pretty face. This guy is in the Gary Cooper tradition—vulnerable, strong, full of integrity and charisma."

—NEW YORK POST, 12/19/84

"Spacek and Gibson give strong performances as a farm couple fighting foreclosure, but they face so many tragedies that their plight verges in parody."

—SATURDAY REVIEW, 1/2/85

"Gibson's baby-faced doggedness and Spacek's ingratiating freckles suit them more for roles as college quarterback and star cheerleader than for hardscrabblers against calamity."

—TIME, 1/17/85

"Gibson's screen persona seems to be regressing with each new role, from would-be Tom Doniphon in Mad Max 2, *through Franchot Tone-as-Fletcher Christian in* The Bounty, *to his latest incarnation here as Paul Bunyan."*

—MONTHLY FILM BULLETIN, 4/85

104

Tom and Mae Garvey and their son, Lewis, work to build a makeshift dam to stop a ravaging river from flooding their farmland.

*T*he *River* is a picturesque drama about a Tennessee farm family's struggle to keep their place from being flooded by the title waterway and taken over by their creditors. And quite a struggle it is. If they're not struggling against the weather, malfunctioning farm equipment, crop blight, the loss of their animals from disease, being too strapped for cash to buy spare parts and seed, suffering on-the-job accidents, and almost bleeding to death for lack of help to call a doctor, they're fighting against the local big shot, Joe Wade, played by Scott Glenn.

It seems Glenn wants to flood their farmland so he can build a dam to irrigate his eleven-thousand acres, a project, it should be noted, that will also bring hydroelectric power and jobs to the impoverished area. He's willing to pay a fair price for the spread, but the stub-

Mae Garvey (Sissy Spacek) isn't as sold on the rigors of farm life as her stubbornly individualistic husband (Mel Gibson) and longs for a better, struggle-free existence.

born patriarch of the family, played by Mel Gibson, isn't interested. "Not lookin' to sell, I'm lookin' to stay," he tells Glenn with prideful laconism. "My people are buried here." Seems the only way he'll leave is in a box, too.

Adding to the tension between the adversaries is Glenn's attraction to Gibson's wife, played by Sissy Spacek. She's not quite as sold on the rigors and rugged individualism of farm life as her husband and longs for a better, struggle-free life. Who can blame her?

Glenn tries to force Gibson out by pressuring the bank to foreclose on the man's property. But Gibson parries by getting a job as a scab at a striking iron-fabrication plant to raise the money to pay the bank.

Spit on by the strikers, he feels ashamed and humiliated and longs to get back to his farm, the film's symbol of all that is wholesome, good, and pure in life, which is restated with heavy-handedness over and over again. For example, at one point, a deer wanders into the

105

they help it escape back to the farmland wilds, where they feel they, too, belong.

When the rains come again and the river swells its banks to threaten Gibson's farm once more, the long-suffering Spacek decides she's had enough and pushes him to give up. Predictably, he refuses, so she tells him to swallow his maverick pride for once and ask help from his friends and neighbors to stem the tide rather than keep the ordeal in the family. He does, and the river is successfully held back. However, having run out of patience with Gibson's stubbornness, Glenn recruits a mob of unemployed locals—some of them Gibson's former scab friends—to break down the barricades and flood the farm for good. But when Gibson stubbornly heads back into the roiling water on his own and plugs the breaks with sandbags, the mob is overcome with shame for its actions and admiration for him. They pitch in to help. Symbolically, they shove greedy Glenn's souped-up Jeep into the water to act as a dam. Licked for now, Glenn muses that the river will get Gibson's farm eventually: "I can wait."

The problem with *The River* is that it's joyless. Not only does this work against our sympathizing very much with the characters; it works against the film's message. Except for a scene of a men's baseball game, nobody in the movie

plant. As Gibson and his fellow scabs lock eyes with the trapped and frightened creature, they have a mystical experience, seeing a reflection of themselves and their own situation. Gently,

Sissy Spacek and Mel Gibson in The River, *Gibson's Hollywood film debut.*

seems to have a moment of fun; even that afore-mentioned moment quickly dissolves into a contest of icy stares and even icier wills between Gibson and Glenn, bitter antagonists to the end, whether on the baseball diamond or off. If the farm is the symbol of life, these people seem to be getting very little out of either but heartache and endless frustration.

Even the Scott Glenn character's wealth seldom makes him smile much. And Mel Gibson doesn't crack his trademark grin once. He's all brooding intensity and righteousness throughout. Frankly, this makes his character a bit of an unsympathetic bore. Why not sell the farm to Glenn and use the money to buy another farm someplace that isn't in constant jeopardy of being submerged? Doesn't this make a great deal of practical sense under the circumstances? And wouldn't it make his family's life a lot easier? By digging in his heels, the character seems more selfish than heroic.

Gibson's statement about phoning in his performance is well taken, although I don't interpret him to mean he sleepwalked through his role. What I think he's saying is that he didn't give the role his all, that he failed to explore other layers of the character that might have made his Tom Garvey more interesting, to him and to us, and by so doing, turned in a rather one note performance. If so, he's right.

On the plus side, however—and it's a *big* plus—the film's photography by Vilmos Zsigmond is gorgeous.

MAD MAX BEYOND THUNDERDOME

1985—WARNER BROS.

*"I don't want to be making this film.
It's just a piece of shit."*

—MEL GIBSON

CREDITS

Producers: George Miller, Doug Mitchell, and Terry Hayes; *Directors:* George Miller and George Ogilvie; *Screenwriters:* Terry Hayes and George Miller; *Cinematographer:* Dean Semler; *Editor:* Richard Francis-Bruce; *Composer:* Maurice Jarre; *Production designer:* Graham Walker.
Running time: 106 minutes.

CAST

Mel Gibson *(Max);* Bruce Spence *(Jedediah the Pilot);* Adam Cockburn *(Jedediah Jr.);* Tina Turner *(Aunty Entity);* Frank Thring *(Collector);* Angelo Rossitto *(Master);* Paul Larsson *(Blaster);* Angry Anderson *(Ironbar);* Robert Grubb *(Pigkiller);* George Spartels *(Blackfinger);* Edwin Hodgeman *(Dr. Dealgood);* Bob Hornery *(Waterseller);* Andrew Oh Ton Ton *(Tattoo);* Helen Buday *(Savannah Nix);* Mark Spain *(Mr. Skyfish).*

REVIEWS

"Mel Gibson, who made his debut [sic] on screen as Max, still packs the old simmering charisma, but he's turned his character toward greater weariness, the deadly equipoise of someone who's danced above hell for too many years—but whose reflexes for heroism (honed in his first incarnation of highway cop defending family) still snaps into place at a challenge."

—LOS ANGELES TIMES, 7/10/85

"In the end the crazy images and unthinkable brutality creates [sic] and communicates [sic] a unique, crude poetry that is both primitive and beautiful. Acting is the last thing on anybody's mind, but Mel Gibson gets through it without smiling."

—NEW YORK POST, 7/10/85

"The high-velocity chases and breathtaking stunts and awesome collisions of the Mad Max *trilogy are worth the price of admission to thrill-seeker and art-lover alike. It is craft raised to art, the contemporary standard of excellence. But Australia's* Mad Max *series is more than a thrillingly choreographed hot rod and motorcycle demolition derby. It is the definitive worst-case scenario in movies today of what life would be like after World War III."*

—NEWSDAY, 7/10/85

Max (Mel Gibson) is back and still governed by the same philosophy: dealing for his wants, then being on his way when the deal is finished.

110

Most series begin to run out of gas by the time they reach the third installment. But *Mad Max Beyond Thunderdome* still has a lot of zip to it, though it offers little that is new about Max or his wasteland universe.

The end of *Mad Max 2: The Road Warrior* found him looking a lot worse for wear than he does here, although his hair is now longer, grayer, and shaggier; in fact, Gibson's appearance is almost a warm-up for his role as William Wallace in *Braveheart,* minus the kilt.

But he's still governed by the old Max philosophy of dealing for his wants, then being on his way once the deal is finished. What he wants in *Beyond Thunderdome* is the scraps of his wrecked V-8. His search for them leads to Bartertown, a hellhole in the middle of the desert with electricity where the price of everything, including radioactive rainwater for the thirsty, comes at a premium.

The place is run by Tina Turner's Aunty Entity, a buffed-up combination of the Acid Queen from The Who's *Tommy* and a female wrestler in leather. She's got labor problems, though. The brainy dwarf nicknamed Master, (Angelo Rossitto), who operates the underground plant that supplies her fiefdom with electricity (produced from methane gas made from pig shit), keeps chipping away at her authority by threatening an embargo. To make Master tow the line, she hires Max to challenge the dwarf's hulky bodyguard, Blaster (Paul Larsson), to a duel to the death in the city's arena, Thunderdome, where the battle cry is "Two men enter, one man leaves." If Max comes out the winner, she'll see to it he gets his car back.

Mixing aerial acrobatics and gladiatorial combat (chainsaw versus spear), the stunningly choreographed duel between Max and Blaster is one of the best action sequences in the series and the highpoint of the film. However, placing this spectacular set piece at the end of the first act rather than climaxing the film with it makes the second act feel even more slow moving than it probably is until things kick into gear again with another high-energy sequence at the finale. But I'm getting ahead of myself.

Max leads a tribe of lost children to the promised land in Mad Max: Beyond Thunderdome.

Max gets the best of Blaster in the arena but refuses to kill him, discovering that the hulk is defenseless when down due to his feeble-mindedness. The decision to go back on his bargain places Max on the outs with Turner, who sends him to a gulag in the desert. There he is rescued by a tribe of lost children (a nod to *Peter Pan* that isn't exactly understated).

In yet another reference to The Who's *Tommy,* the children believe that Max is their savior, Captain Walker, the pilot who was flying them to a place of salvation called Tomorrow-morrowland until their plane crashed and he was killed. They want Max to finish the job and get them there. But Max wants neither the idolatry nor the responsibility and turns them down. When some of the kids set out on their own, he realizes they'll run smack into Barter-town and get swallowed up in its morass of violence and immorality.

Leading the rest of the kids, he goes to find them and deliver the entire tribe to Tomor-row-morrowland, after all. His efforts lead to a spectacular high-speed chase through the desert involving planes, trains, and automobiles—as kinetic a crashfest as the road-action scenes in the other *Mad Max* movies, where such scenes were nonstop. However, some fans of the series may be disappointed because it's the only one in the movie and comes so near the end.

Max sacrifices his own safety to rescue the kids and Master from Turner's cutthroats. Vaguely reprising his role as the Gyro Captain in *Mad Max 2,* itinerant pilot Bruce Spence flies the group to Tomorrow-morrowland in his battered aircraft to rebuild civilization with Master's guidance. Again, Gibson, as Max, paves the way for someone else to get the job done.

It looks like curtains for the trapped Max. But having developed a deep respect for her adversary, Turner lets him go with a wry "Raggedy man, ain't we a pair?"

We last see Max wandering across the burning sand under the hot sun like the lost Gasim in *Lawrence of Arabia*—just one of many homages the film pays to David Lean's 1962 desert classic, including replacing *Road Warrior* composer Brian May with *Lawrence* composer Maurice Jarre to supply the music score.

Aunty Entity (Tina Turner), the deadly ruler of Barter-
town, leads her imperial guards against Max in a chase
through the desert.

LETHAL WEAPON

1987—WARNER BROS.

"I pictured Riggs as an almost Chaplinesque figure, a guy who doesn't expect anything from life and even toys with the idea of taking his own. He's not like these stalwarts who come down from Mt. Olympus and wreak havoc and go away. He's somebody who doesn't look like he's set to go off until he actually does."

—MEL GIBSON

CREDITS

Producers: Richard Donner and Joel Silver; *Director:* Richard Donner; *Screenwriter:* Shane Black; *Cinematographer:* Stephen Goldblatt; *Editor:* Stuart Baird; *Composers:* Michael Kamen and Eric Clapton; *Production designer:* J. Michael Riva.
Running time: 110 minutes.

CAST

Mel Gibson *(Martin Riggs);* Danny Glover *(Roger Murtaugh);* Gary Busey *(Joshua);* Mitchell Ryan *(General);* Tom Atkins *(Michael Hunsaker);* Darlene Love *(Trish Murtaugh);* Traci Wolfe *(Rianne Murtaugh);* Jackie Swanson *(Amanda Hunsaker);* Damon Hines *(Nick Murtaugh);* Ebonie Smith *(Carrie Murtaugh);* Lycia Naff *(Dixie);* Selma Archerd *(Policewoman);* Patrick Cameron *(Police detective);* Don Gordon *(Police detective);* Richard B. Whitaker *(Police officer).*

REVIEWS

"Gibson and Glover are such good actors that as long as the camera stays on them—and not on the slicked-up, empty Hollywood carnage exploding predictably around them—the movie is fun."

—LOS ANGELES TIMES, 3/6/87

"Gibson's Australian accent intrudes occasionally, making it hard to believe he's really a Californian. But he's just as credible a hero against overwhelming odds in Lethal Weapon *as he has been in all three* Mad Max *pictures."*

—NEWSDAY, 3/6/87

"Riggs is [Mad] Max's *psychological cousin, a man whose wild-eyed courage is based on having witnessed so much cruelty that he no longer cares whether he lives or dies. Gibson knows just how to temper the gaga energy of such figures with odd bursts of sweet innocence."*

—TIME, 3/27/87

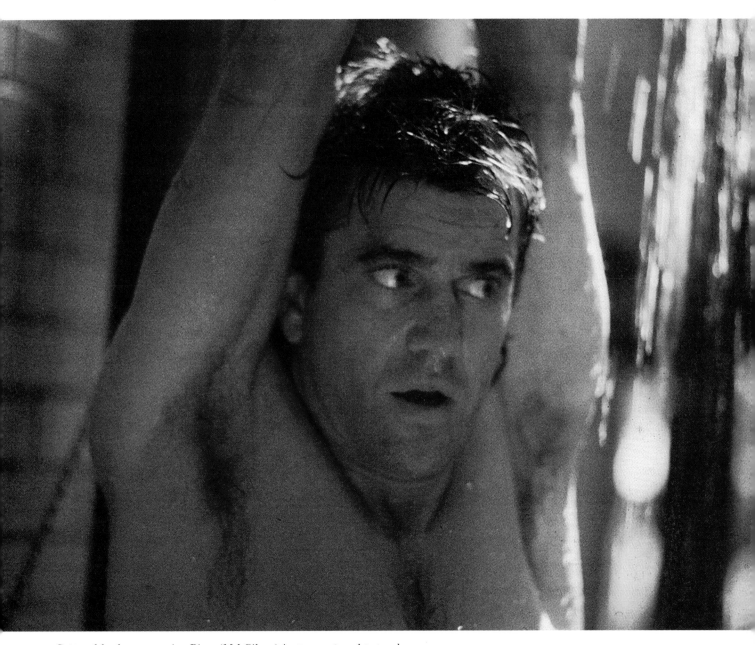

Captured by the mercenaries, Riggs (Mel Gibson) is strung up and tortured.

"Gibson's moony performance as a suicidal, devil-may-care Los Angeles cop is the best thing in this absurdly violent, poorly plotted movie, which has been overpraised from coast to coast."

—NEW YORK, 4/6/87

"Gibson, as Riggs, displays a wide range of emotions, from tears to terror. He registers every nuance of feeling, hammers home his physical strength and intensity and smoothly juxtaposes his semi-psychotic persona with wry humor."

—FILMS IN REVIEW, 5/87

The final shot in *Mad Max Beyond Thunderdome* of the hero wandering across the desert left us wondering if we would ever see Max again.

Given Mel Gibson's reported disdain for the film, this seems unlikely. As enjoyable as that third entry in the series was on many levels, it was really one *Mad Max* movie too many as far as the character was concerned. By the end of the second installment, *Mad Max 2: The Road Warrior,* we had learned all there was to know about Max. Here Gibson was just walking the

(1973)—and every other cop picture ever made.

But in the character of one of the script's protagonists, Martin Riggs, a cop mourning the death of his wife to the point of suicide, Gibson apparently found what he was looking for—a chance to dig deep into an area of the Max character not possible with Max himself. For here was a Mad Max who truly was mad, who *had* slipped over the edge, who really *didn't* seem to care whether he lived or died, who *was* spinning violently out of control, yet is finally brought back from the abyss by a human connection.

Our first view of Gibson's Martin Riggs establishes the character's similarity to Max and, at the same time, difference from him.

Riggs, too, is a widower, a cop, and a loner, his only companion a dog. But Riggs has given *his* dog a name, a

character over old ground. Max wasn't even "mad" anymore; he'd become just a lone leading man dressed in rags.

In point of fact, Max never really was "mad" in the clinical sense. He was angry and vengeful but too self-controlled and calculating to ever slip over the edge into outright psychosis. This is probably why the script of *Lethal Weapon* appealed so strongly to Gibson. He says he turned a lot of action scripts down in the wake of *Beyond Thunderdome* because they lacked something he was looking for. The script itself isn't much more than a rehash of elements from Clint Eastwood's first two *Dirty Harry* movies—*Dirty Harry* (1971) and *Magnum Force*

subtle indicator that even in his despair he still seeks attachment and hasn't completely turned his back on life. He still has hope, though it might not seem so as he slugs down a bottle of beer for breakfast.

We next see Riggs taking down a bunch of drug dealers, a bust that gets dangerously out of hand largely because of Riggs himself; he pushes the dealers too far with some Three Stooges–type taunts and acts of humiliation (a Gibson touch for sure).

As cops swarm the place, one of the drug dealers gets the drop on Riggs, puts a gun to his head, and orders the cops back or he'll shoot. Crazily, Riggs badgers the dealer to go ahead, a bluff that works—except it wasn't a bluff. Riggs meant it, and the look in his eyes moments later as he gets his adrenaline and emotions back under control reveals he scared himself, too.

This leads to the electrifying scene described elsewhere in this book in which the unstable Riggs contemplates taking his own life rather than pushing a surrogate into doing it for him.

Gazing with loneliness and drunken anguish at a photo of his dead wife (who was killed in a road accident, much like Max's spouse), he realizes he can't pull the trigger. He may be self-destructive, but the hunger for life still burns somewhere within him. "I'll see you later," he tells the woman in the photo softly, with tears in his eyes. "Much later."

These intense glimpses into the character's grieving, desperate soul were denied us with Max. Gibson brings both scenes off—each offering a very different type of glimpse, the first public, the second private—with credibility and power. Furthermore, he sustains the character's believable and terrifying unpredictability throughout the film, shifting mercurially between mood swings of comic craziness and pathological violence with a deftness matched in the movies by only one other actor, Jack Nicholson. Had

Gibson's performance as the violent, reckless Riggs elevates the routine action-drama Lethal Weapon *into a forceful character study.*

117

Lethal Weapon been a straight drama and not an action movie, Gibson's remarkable performance as Riggs would probably have earned him an Oscar nomination as Best Actor.

Transferred from the vice squad to homicide division because of his irrational behavior during the drug bust, Riggs is teamed with older cop Roger Murtaugh, played by Danny Glover.

Director Richard Donner and Mel Gibson on the set of Lethal Weapon.

118

Like Dirty Harry, Det. Martin Riggs (Mel Gibson) gets all the dirty jobs. Here he tries to talk a jumper (Michael Shaner) out of committing suicide by pushing him into it and even joining him.

A stable family man with a house in the suburbs, Murtaugh is looking forward to an imminent, comfortable retirement—a prospect the loose cannon Riggs continually jeopardizes by getting them into one near-death scrape after another. The uncertain relationship eventually proves to be Riggs's salvation, for the two men grow to trust and rely on one another.

The script doesn't give Danny Glover much to build his character on other than variations of the line "I'm too old for this shit" whenever Gibson gets them into trouble. But the chemistry between the two actors is real and affecting and gives the relationship its foundation and substance.

Still, it is Mel Gibson's performance as the tormented Riggs that elevates what is otherwise an exciting, if routine, action melodrama into a forceful character study as well.

TEQUILA SUNRISE

1988—WARNER BROS.

"When I first read [the script of] Tequila Sunrise, *I thought, well, What was that? But I kept reading it. And I thought, I've got to read that again. That's what the film is like. You think, What is going on here? And then it just sucks you in."*

—MEL GIBSON

CREDITS

Producer: Thom Mount; *Director:* Robert Towne; *Screenwriter:* Robert Towne; *Cinematographer:* Conrad Hall; *Editor:* Claire Simpson; *Composer:* Dave Grusin; *Production designer:* Richard Sylbert.
Running time: 116 minutes.

CAST

Mel Gibson *(Dale McKussic);* Kurt Russell *(Lt. Nick Frescia);* Michelle Pfeiffer *(Jo Ann Vallenari);* Raul Julia *(Escalante);* J. T. Walsh *(Maguire);* Arliss Howard *(Gregg Lindroff);* Ann Magnuson *(Shaleen);* Arye Gross *(Andy Leonard);* Gabriel Damon *(Cody McKussic);* Garret Pearson *(Arturo);* Eric Thiele *(Vittorio);* Tom Nolan *(Leland);* Dawn Martel *(Sin Sister);* Lala *(Sin Sister No. 2);* Budd Boetticher *(Judge Nizetitch).*

REVIEWS

"Gibson's [blue eyes] burn, their color in contrast to the blackness of his soul. Steady and gentle as he is, there's also something coiled in him—his softness has a scary, exciting edge. He's like Henry Fonda with the madness closer to the surface."

—NEW YORK POST, 12/2/88

"It's odd that Gibson's character never has an edge of danger about him. But it's nice to see the actor have the chance to play balmy bemusement—he does it so engagingly."

—LOS ANGELES TIMES, 12/2/88

"Mel Gibson is a consummate actor. He has the range and depth to make Mac a sympathetic character despite his past. His Mac is haunted by his history, paranoid about his present, and conscious of his future. These traits merge in Gibson's seamless performance to create an honorable ex–bad guy."

—FILMS IN REVIEW, 4/89

Costars Mel Gibson, Kurt Russell, and Michelle Pfeiffer. Gibson had the most challenging part; Russell, the best role.

121

A celebrated French director once noted that when actors become stars, they often become so afraid of losing their position that they refuse to try something new and choose only those roles that ensure the audience will keep loving them. Not so Mel Gibson, who, as we've seen, often selects parts on the basis of the challenge they present in sustaining the audience's affection.

This was the case as well in Robert Towne's romantic crime drama *Tequila Sunrise*. Gibson took on the unsavory role of a drug dealer after many of Hollywood's other top male stars passed on it. Gibson himself had declined such roles for many years not because he was afraid of losing the audience's affection but because he found such characters morally offensive to him personally. But the role of drug dealer Dale McKussic in *Tequila Sunrise* was different in that the character was trying to go straight but no one would let him.

The DEA wants to nail McKussic for his past crimes as well as lead them to an even bigger fish. His former associates in the drug trade—like Gibson's Mexican connection (Raul Julia), a kingpin cloaked in anonymity, known to author-

McKussic keeps a protective eye on his son during a day at the beach in Tequila Sunrise, *a jigsaw puzzle of hidden agendas, power games, and complex relationships.*

ities only as "Carlos"—don't want him to quit because he was such a moneymaker for them. His customers don't want to have to find another supplier. His ex-wife needs money to replace the expensive family car she's just wrecked. He's got a child to support, and he's having a difficult time making ends meet.

With all this pressure to keep raking in the loot dealing drugs, "It's harder to get out than you think," he confesses to the girl he's fallen in love with, a beautiful restaurateur, Jo Ann (played by Michelle Pfeiffer) he'd been hesitant to reveal his feelings to for fear her knowledge of his past would occasion a rebuff.

Instead, she falls in love with him a situation the DEA and the L.A. narcotics squad use to their advantage by pressuring her to funnel information to them so they can take McKussic and his phantom Mexican connection down. To further complicate things, Lt. Nick Frescia, the head of the narcotics squad, played by Kurt Russell, is a longtime friend of McKussic's who has fallen for Pfeiffer himself.

As the plot snakes its way through a labyrinth of quirky twists, turns, and seemingly unfathomable character motivations and relationships, we wonder just how the romantic triangle and all the various side issues will eventually be resolved. Is Pfeiffer the innocent bystander she seems to be, or does she have a shadier side, too? Will she choose Gibson or Russell? Is Gibson really trying to get out of the drug business or just pretending? Is Russell actually in love with Pfeiffer or just using her to make a big-time drug bust that will advance his career? Is Russell Gibson's friend or foe? Who's the snitch that keeps the DEA breathing down Gibson's neck? Who is Carlos, what's the nature of his friendship with Gibson, and will Gibson turn his back on that friendship and hand Carlos over?

What writer-director Towne was aiming for here, I think, was a jigsaw puzzle of contemporary hidden agendas, power games, and complex relationships on the order of his period

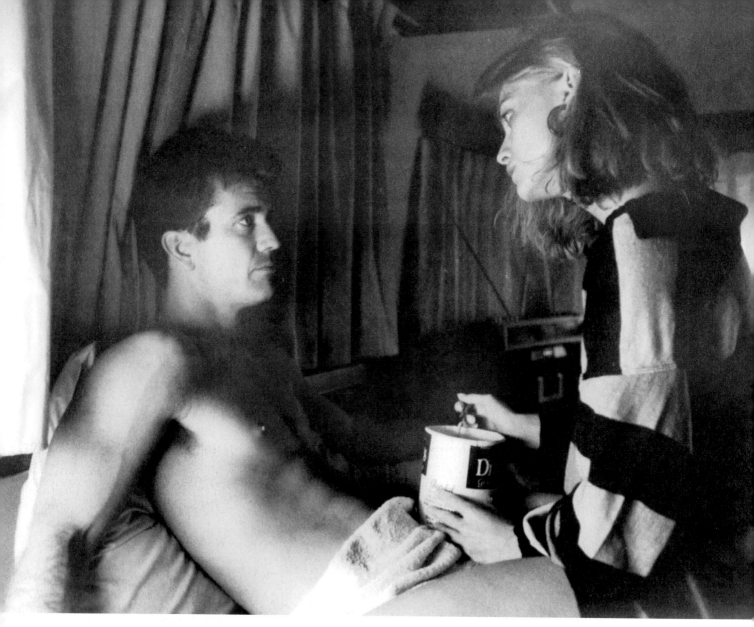

Pressured to keep raking in the loot dealing drugs, McKussic confesses, "It's harder to get out than you think," to his upstanding girlfriend Jo Ann (Pfeiffer).

neonoir masterwork *Chinatown* (1974). But after a promising start in which the pieces of the puzzle are intriguingly placed before us, the film strives so hard to keep us guessing where they will lead and how they will all fit together that the movie becomes confusing and runs out of steam.

Even more problematic is that despite all the plot machinations, the story itself is quite thin. In the end, the questions raised about the characters turn out to be more compelling than the ho-hum answers that are provided.

Towne has long been one of Hollywood's most sought after script doctors; his script for *Tequila Sunrise* could have used a little of that

medical attention also. It draws us in, and the film's star power keeps us watching, but the payoff is rather weak.

Fortunately, the film has plenty of the required star power in its three charismatic leads. Gibson successfully conveys the turmoil of the ex–drug dealer haunted by his past, although the motives behind McKussic's determination to retire from the drug trade and suddenly go straight after so many years aren't really explored except to say he feels he's been operating on borrowed time. It's up to Gibson to fill in most of the blanks of his underwritten part, and he does.

His McKussic comes across as a man constantly on the edge, always looking over his shoulder to see who's after him; even when alone with Pfeiffer, as in the film's steamy hot-tub love scene, he speaks in a low-keyed, hesitant manner, as if suspecting someone is listening in. He jokes about his paranoia while, in the same breath, acknowledging the legitimate reasons for it. That we side with McKussic as much as we do is largely because Gibson successfully met the challenge of making us like and care about the somewhat unsavory character.

Pfeiffer is not only gorgeous to look at but is given a more complex role than Gibson as the woman torn between the two friends who is constantly shifting alliances until she follows her heart.

But the film's most complex and fascinating character is Kurt Russell's manipulative Lieutenant Frescia. All smiles and cunning, he's the only character who has a clear understanding of himself and everyone else and always seems to know what's going on.

In the end, this may have been the most difficult challenge *Tequila Sunrise* presented Mel Gibson: keeping his character alive on-screen opposite Russell's Lieutenant Frescia, the film's best role and the guy the picture is really all about.

A man on the edge, always looking over his shoulder to see who's after him.

125

LETHAL WEAPON 2

1989—WARNER BROS.

"It's just horsing around . . . that's the spirit of [director Richard] Donner. He's like a big kid."

CREDITS

Producers: Richard Donner, Joel Silver, Steve Perry, and Jennie Lew Tugend; *Director:* Richard Donner; *Screenwriter:* Jeffrey Boam, based on a story by Shane Black and Warren Murphy and on characters created by Black; *Cinematographer:* Stephen Goldblatt; *Editor:* Stuart Baird; *Composers:* Michael Kamen, Eric Clapton, and David Sanborn; *Production designer:* J. Michael Riva. Running time: 113 minutes.

CAST

Mel Gibson *(Martin Riggs);* Danny Glover *(Roger Murtaugh);* Joe Pesci *(Leo Getz);* Joss Ackland *(Arjen Rudd);* Derrick O'Connor *(Pieter Vorstedt);* Patsy Kensit *(Rika van den Haas);* Darlene Love *(Trish Murtaugh);* Traci Wolfe *(Rianne Murtaugh);* Steve Kahan *(Captain Murphy);* Mark Rolston *(Hans);* Jenette Goldstein *(Meagan Shapiro);* Dean Norris *(Tim Cavanaugh);* Juney Smith *(Tom Wyler);* Nestor Serrano *(Eddie Estaban);* Damon Hines *(Nick Murtaugh);* Ebonie Smith *(Carrie Murtaugh).*

REVIEWS

"The movie has a bouncy, comic-book appeal: sadism has never been so good-natured. The secret, in addition to Pesci's bravura turn, is in the interplay between the volatile Gibson and the kinder, gentler Glover, who are more fun to watch together now that they don't have to pretend they don't get along."

—*NEWSWEEK, 7/17/89*

"Mel Gibson, in and out of the buff, gives his loosest, goosiest performance yet."

—*NEW YORK, 8/7/89*

"Gibson gives a solid performance. Again, Gibson's range allows him the luxury of fully realizing and displaying tragic emotions."

—*FILMS IN REVIEW, 10/89*

Audiences hoping to see Riggs, the lethal weapon, explode with even greater force in the sequel were not disappointed.

Back in action: Mel Gibson as Martin Riggs and Danny Glover as Roger Murtaugh in Lethal Weapon 2.

The opening-title music, a variation of the Warner Bros. Looney Tunes theme, perfectly sets the tone for this zany follow-up to the hugely popular *Lethal Weapon. That* film had plenty of laughs, but there was drama and poignancy to the Riggs-Murtaugh relationship, too. Here the emphasis of the film and the relationship is mainly on wildly over-the-top action and slapstick humor in the tradition of Bugs Bunny, the Road Runner, and of course, the Three Stooges.

Although Riggs's emotional problems were substantially resolved by the conclusion of *Lethal Weapon,* the sequel finds him as out of control as ever—maybe even more so. And he's driving Murtaugh, now that much closer to retirement, to even greater desperation by the constant perils in which he keeps placing them.

When the lives of Murtaugh and his family are threatened by thugs connected to a drug case he and Riggs are working on, the partners are reassigned to watch over the state's star witness in an unrelated money-laundering case. Eventually, the two cases become linked.

Some shady South African diplomats have cornered the L.A. drug market, their profits laundered by the very witness Riggs and Murtaugh have been assigned to protect—an endearing, motormouthed little goofball, Leo Getz, played by Joe Pesci. He assumes the role of Curly, to Gibson and Glover's Moe and Larry, respectively (although Gibson occasionally mimics Curly's persona as well). The scenes between them, with Pesci serving as the butt of

Riggs gets a love interest (Rika, played by Patsy Kensit), whose shocking fate ties back to the death of his first wife and ignites his fuse with a vengeance.

most of the jokes, generate the film's biggest laughs, which is undoubtedly why Pesci's character was brought back for, arguably, the even more Stooges-like sequel, *Lethal Weapon 3*. After all, you can't have a Three Stooges movie without Curly.

The sequel doesn't ignore the poignant side of the Riggs-Murtaugh relationship, however. In fact, the bond between the two of them is even stronger. This is nicely illustrated in the scene in which Murtaugh, having sent his wife and kids to live with relatives until the heat blows over, retreats to the family bathroom to relieve himself and relax with a sailing magazine, only to discover the bad guys have booby-trapped his toilet to explode if he stands up.

When Murtaugh doesn't show up for work or answer his phone, Riggs senses trouble, heads for Murtaugh's home, finds him trapped on the toilet, and calls in the bomb squad (although Murtaugh, caught literally with his pants down, had asked Riggs to keep things quiet).

The squad is unable to defuse the bomb

The bad guys ready the weighted-down Riggs for a deadly dunk in the ocean. But he's a hard man to keep down.

Murtaugh steps in to help his bloodied pal, who was shot up badly while taking out the villains before they could escape to South Africa.

but can delay the detonator a few seconds, enough time for Murtaugh to jump free. The problem is that Murtaugh can't move; his legs are numb from sitting on the can for so many hours. Placing his own life in jeopardy, Riggs stays behind to pull his friend clear at the critical time into the cast-iron bathtub. Linking hands as they count nervously to three, they lock eyes to ease each other's terror, silently communicating their friendship and respect for each other in what could be their final moments. All goes well, of course. In fact, the payoff is quite funny. But the scene is tense nonetheless and ultimately quite moving due to the chemistry between Gibson and Glover and the conviction they bring to their roles.

Audiences hoping to see the lethal weapon, Riggs, explode with even greater force this time around won't be disappointed. He gets a love interest whose shocking fate ties back to the death of his wife in a surprise twist that ignites with a vengeance his already short fuse.

In the film's spectacular climax—actually there are two of them—Riggs gets even with some of the bad guys by bringing their house quite literally down around their ears, then gets shot up pretty badly trying to take out the rest of the gang before they set sail to South Africa with their laundered loot. At the same time, Murtaugh steps in, of course, to help his bloodied pal finish them off with a violent flourish—and close the case on a note of laughter and good-natured ribbing, in the spirit of *Lethal Weapon 2.*

AIR AMERICA

1990—CAROLCO

"It isn't a perfect film. A lot of things aren't right with it, but it's okay."

—MEL GIBSON

CREDITS

Producers: Mario Kassar, Daniel Melnick, and Andrew G. Vajna; *Director:* Roger Spottiswoode; *Screenwriters:* John Eskow, Richard Rush, and Fernando Trueba; *Cinematographer:* Roger Deakins; *Editors:* John Bloom and Lois Freeman-Cox; *Composer:* Charles Gross; *Production designer:* Allan Cameron.
Running time: 112 minutes.

CAST

Mel Gibson *(Gene Ryack);* Robert Downey Jr. *(Billy Covington);* Nancy Travis *(Corinne Landreaux);* David Marshall Grant *(Rob Diehl);* Lane Smith *(Senator Davenport);* Ken Jenkins *(Maj. Donald Lemond);* Burt Kwouk *(Gen. Lu Soong);* Art La Fleur *(Jack Neely);* Tim Thomerson *(Babo);* Marshall Bell *(O.V.);* David Bowe *(Saunders);* Burke Byrnes *(Recruiter);* Ned Eisenberg *(Pirelli);* Sinjai Hongthai *(Gene's Wife);* Harvey Jason *(Nino).*

REVIEWS

"Mel Gibson gives a cocky, assured performance—a star performance. But he doesn't provide the kind of shadowings that make Gene's guilt-ridden con-artist resonate."

—LOS ANGELES TIMES, 8/10/90

"Gibson, in the sleaze role, eases his way through—a dry, expert turn, if an unexciting one."

—NEW YORK POST, 8/10/90

"Regardless of any incipient torment in his soul, Gibson maintains an almost preturnatural calm in episode after episode of high jinks aloft."

—NEWSDAY, 8/10/90

"Quick-tongued, with eyes that light up the sky, Mel Gibson is the heart of Air America—*and the element that throws it off course. He's an ironist in a cynical world, a romantic hero trapped in an interminable* Saturday Night Live *skit and trying to be a good sport about it."*

—VILLAGE VOICE, 8/21/90

The script softens Ryack's cynicism, never quite allowing the character the courage of his lack of convictions.

Air America is a genial but unexceptional comedy-satire about a serious subject: covert U.S. military and drug-running operations in Laos during the Vietnam War.

In *Lethal Weapon*, Mel Gibson went up against a shadow company of ex-CIA spooks, trained killers, and mercenaries who once ran heroin out of Laos via Air America, then transferred their illegal operations stateside with the coming of peacetime. Here Gibson's character,

Gene Ryack, is on the opposite side. As one of the pilots for the CIA-supported Air America, he's being used by the same shadowy types to do the drug running.

The year is 1969, the height of the Vietnam War. North Vietnamese troops are spilling over the border into Laos to build supply lines in response to U.S. bombing. To avoid the appearance of widening the war but to stem the Communist tide, the United States sends

combat troops into Laos in secret, using the CIA-backed Air America to transport weapons, men, food, and supplies in and out of the country.

A deal is struck with a Laotian general named Soong (played by Burt Kwouk of *Pink Panther* fame) to support the counterinsurgency effort with troops of his own; in exchange, the CIA not only turns a blind eye to the general's drug-running activities but allows him to use Air

who are among the biggest consumers of these drugs, Ryack and his flier pals mask whatever guilt or responsibility they may feel over their involvement with well-honed cynicism. A screwball version of the tight-knit group of fliers in *The Dawn Patrol* (1938), they're just trouble junkies mainlining on danger who respect only each other; the only cause they care about is their own.

We know nothing of Ryack's background—how or why he came to be hired to work for Air America; all we know about him is that he's gone native and aims to retire to a farm in Thailand with his Laotian wife and family, a dream he plans to finance by scoring big with a stockpile of stolen weapons he's been hoarding.

When a buffoonish but honest U.S. senator (Lane Smith) arrives on a fact-finding mission to see how the covert operation is going, military officials are careful to keep the drug-running activities from him. Acknowledging the tight political squeeze their country has put them in, the senator dishes out some patriotic appreciation to the fliers: "We know what you boys are doing here," he says. "Good," they drunkenly respond, "Explain it to us."

Enter Billy Covington (Robert Downey Jr.), a former eye-in-the-sky traffic reporter for an L.A. radio station who was grounded out of a job, then recruited by the CIA to put his flying talents to work for Air America. The new recruit is taken aback by the near-psychotic behavior of his fellow pilots until the more easygoing Ryack takes him under his wing. The duo get into several male-bonding scrapes together, including a run-in with some guerrillas who shoot their chopper down. Captured and threatened with execution, Ryack smoothly hustles them out of the dilemma by trading some of his stockpiled guns for their lives.

Though not especially patriotic, Covington soon becomes the conscience of the duo. He is appalled by the CIA's morally repugnant drug-running activities. "Until I worked for the government, I never, never smuggled dope," he

America to ship the drugs throughout Southeast Asia—provided he kicks back some of the profits to fund the CIA's Laotian operation.

Even though the drug trafficking is having a destructive effect on U.S. troops in Vietnam,

Ryack and Covington's (Downey Jr.) chopper is shot down by guerrillas.

tells Ryack, upbraiding him for his cynical complicity.

The insanity of it all hits home when Covington is shot down again and the shipment of drugs stashed on his crippled plane is saved by General Soong before he and his crew are. Now furious as well as appalled, he attempts to right the wrongs he sees by blowing up the general's drug-processing plant. But it's up and running again within a couple of hours.

When the visiting senator finally gets wind of the drug operation and angrily demands that the bad apples involved be ferreted out and severely punished, the general and his CIA cronies set Covington up to take the fall. He skillfully evades entrapment, however, and the senator comes to realize that Covington and his fellow fliers aren't the bad apples; their superiors are. He's powerless to bring them up on charges, though, because the government can't acknowledge any presence in Laos.

Eventually, enemy troops close in on the general's poppy fields, where the refugee population is also located. Air America is conscripted to evacuate all drugs, weapons, and military personnel, but not the doomed refugees. Ryack loads his stockpile of guns aboard his plane, determined to get out while the going's good. But Covington challenges him to be altruistic for once in his

life and help the refugees instead.

Ryack destroys the guns so that no one can get their hands on them and flies the refugees out, his dreams of an easy retirement seemingly going up in smoke by his act of redemption, along with the guns. But the wily Ryack has an ace up his sleeve. He sells the U.S.-owned plane to recoup his losses, knowing the government can't come after him because officially the craft can't exist, and retires to Thailand on schedule.

Mel Gibson strikes the right note of amused insolence as the charming hustler but fails to convince us of the character's cynicism because the script keeps pulling its punches to soften his edge. He may shrug off the moral insanity going on around him with caustic remarks like "If you can't laugh at war, what the hell use is fighting it," but he's never allowed the courage of his lack of convictions. In the end, his "nest egg versus refugees" decision carries little moral weight because he makes it so quickly and easily that one feels he never gave it a single self-serving thought. It loses its redemptive power because there's nothing to redeem. Even the Covington character remarks, "That was fast!"

Covington's idealism is similarly tempered. He's supposed to be the film's conscience, but the script never allows him to express any righteous indignation. He seems more bewildered and amused than morally outraged

137

Ryack plans to score big so he can retire to a farm in Thailand with his Laotian wife and family.

by the wrongs going on around him. His decisions to right them seem almost whimsical, like an afterthought or merely something to do. They have no conviction. Ironically, this makes the character come across as more genuinely cynical than Ryack.

The script went through so many revisions to tip the balance from biting satire and harsh indictment to zany comedy that it wound up having no spine. Even the laughs are subdued. The flying sequences are exciting, however; the crashes, spectacular.

Gibson and Downey Jr. in Air America, *a genial but unexceptional comedy-satire about a serious and controversial subject, CIA drug-running activities in Laos.*

BIRD ON A WIRE

1990—UNIVERSAL

"I didn't realize I was that furry on my back end. My bum's got a fair carpet, doesn't it?"

—MEL GIBSON

CREDITS

Producers: Rob Cohen, Robert W. Cort, and Ted Field; *Director:* John Badham; *Screenwriters:* Eric Lerner, David Seltzer, and Louis Venosta; *Cinematographer:* Robert Primes; *Editors:* Frank Morriss and Dallas Pruett; *Composer:* Hans Zimmer; *Production designer:* Philip Harrison.
Running time: 110 minutes.

CAST

Mel Gibson *(Rick Jarmin);* Goldie Hawn *(Marianne Graves);* David Carradine *(Eugene Sorenson);* Bill Duke *(Albert Diggs);* Stephen Tobolowsky *(Joe Weyburn);* Joan Severance *(Rachel Varney);* Jeff Corey *(Lou Baird);* Michel Barbe *(Maitre d');* Alex Brushananski *(Raun);* Jackson Davies *(Paul Bernard);* Leslie Ewen *(Night Receptionist);* Oscar Goncalves *(Bank Guard);* Tim Healy *(Paul);* Paul Jarrett *(Carl Laemmle);* Doug Judge *(Cop at Café).*

REVIEWS

"Has a male star ever received this much on-camera ogling at the expense of his female costar? Goldie Hawn flounces around in a series of unflattering poses while Gibson—literally—butts into half of his scenes. There's a fanny joke around every corner."

—LOS ANGELES TIMES, 5/18/90

"Swaggering, happy-go-lucky, with a broad American accent, Gibson seems charmed. It's an ego-trip part."

—NEW YORK POST, 5/18/90

"The ever-appealing, if slightly plumpish, Gibson seems to relish an unattended motorcycle or skydiving plane more than he does being with her [Goldie Hawn]."

—VILLAGE VOICE, 5/22/90

"Gibson has developed a comic style in silly action pictures that is itself a pleasure to watch and that transcends the movies. Fast as a leopard yet loose

The desperate duo utilizes every available means of transportation to elude the killers hot on their trail.

and goony, Gibson startles the other characters with his quickness. He has become an intensely physical actor, showing just enough of what's inside him to be a great tease."

—*NEW YORK, 5/28/90*

Bird on a Wire is one of those movies that must have seemed good on paper, but apparently something got lost in the translation from script to screen; otherwise, it's hard to imagine why so many big-name talents would have wanted to get involved.

Striking one of his few serious poses in Bird on a Wire, *a film that unsuccessfully tries to recall the screwball comedies of the 1930s.*

The film attempts to recall the classic screwball comedies of the 1930s, like Howard Hawks's *Bringing Up Baby* (1938), with Mel Gibson and Goldie Hawn reversing the Cary Grant and Katharine Hepburn roles. Here she's the conservative character about to marry a dullard who has her staid, unromantic lifestyle turned wildly upside down. He's the wild thing who gets her to cut loose and have fun again, though she never quite seems to know what's going on.

The lure of irresponsibility which binds them together is that he's on the run from the mob; she's an old flame who has a chance encounter with him just as his Witness Protection Program identity gets blown. Both were 1960s antiwar activists. On the verge of marrying, they suddenly took different paths. He

141

142

went to Mexico with a buddy to score some drugs, got mixed up with some corrupt DEA agents, saw them commit a murder, and disappeared into the federal Witness Protection Program in exchange for his testimony against one of the killers. Why he didn't testify against the other killer at the same time is one of the many loopholes in the contrived plot which the screenwriters conveniently ignore in order to give the plot its impetus.

Believing Gibson to be dead but never having gotten him out of her system, Goldie went on to become that symbol of the establishment, a hotshot lawyer. Now the jailed DEA thug, Sorenson (David Carradine), has been paroled. Aided by a corrupt official with access to the Witness Protection Program files, Carradine and the other killer, Albert Diggs (Bill Duke), set out to murder Mel before he can testify against Duke, too. Thrown together with her former lover by coincidence, Goldie becomes a target also. They laugh, shriek, and make love through one hairbreadth escape after another by car, motorcycle, and airplane. Frenetic action quickly overtakes farce, culminating in a spectacular fight scene set in a high-tech zoo where the two former peaceniks dispatch their foes with guns and electricity.

Sandwiched between the relentless smashups, gunplay, and PG-13 bloodshed is an array of leering sight gags, puns, sexy comments, and off-color jokes about Mel's butt and/or Goldie's. When their airplane is shot down by the bad guys in a pursuing helicopter, he advises her what to do when the plane crashes with that oldest of jokes: "Bend over, put your head between your knees, and kiss your butt goodbye." Even the baboons at the zoo fail to escape the filmmakers' almost obsessive fixation with this particular part of the anatomy. While Gibson's *Braveheart* would eventually set the record for the most bare butts to appear in a movie in a single scene, *Bird on a Wire* surely holds the record for the most butt references in a single film.

Crass fun is poked elsewhere, too. In a scene in which macho Mel pretends he's gay

Mel and Goldie take a precarious route to safety in a film with more fanny jokes and references than any movie on record.

Mel and Goldie find themselves one step ahead of the law and some ruthless criminals.

with unrestrained, stereotypical swishiness, the filmmakers score a couple of points for thumbing their noses at political correctness, but they quickly wind up in the debit column because the scene is so witless. And a plot twist involving Alzheimer's disease that's intended to add suspense and irony also falls tastelessly flat.

Goldie Hawn has a definite flair for comedy, but her incessant, ear-splitting displays of ditzy panic are more grating than funny here. Mel Gibson has a flair for comedy, too; strangely, it seldom gets a good showcase in his outright comedies, where it mostly comes across as mugging. As is the case in *Bird on a Wire*.

HAMLET

1990—WARNER BROS.

"The man [Hamlet] is a livin' bomb, and that's how I decided to play him."
—MEL GIBSON

CREDITS

Producer: Lovell Dyson; *Director:* Franco Zeffirelli;
Screenwriters: Christopher DeVore, and Franco Zeffirelli,
based on the play by William Shakespeare;
Cinematographer: David Watkin; *Editor:* Richard Marden;
Composer: Ennio Morricone;
Production designer: Dante Ferretti.
Running time: 135 minutes.

CAST

Mel Gibson *(Hamlet);* Glenn Close *(Gertrude);* Alan Bates
(King Claudius); Paul Scofield *(Ghost);* Ian Holm
(Polonius); Helena Bonham Carter *(Ophelia);* Stephan
Dillan *(Horatio);* Nathaniel Parker *(Laertes);* Sean Murray
(Guildenstern); Michael Maloney *(Rosencrantz);* Trevor
Peacock *(Gravedigger);* John McEnery *(Osric);* Richard
Warwick *(Bernardo);* Christien Anholt *(Marcellus);*
Dave Duffy *(Francisco).*

REVIEWS

"Yes, Mel Gibson makes a good Hamlet. By my troth, a very good Hamlet, and it's a doubly pleasant surprise, since all we've had to judge him by are the likes of Mad Max *and* Lethal Weapon, *in which dilemmas are more easily resolved with fisticuffs than with soliloquy."*
—NEW YORK POST, 12/19/90

"As Hamlet, Gibson embellishes his hunky-charming repertoire by playing hunky-depressive. His readings are clear, low-key morose and as far as that goes, he's always good without being terribly interesting."
—NEWSDAY, 12/19/90

"How does Mel rate? Well, let's give him a B. He's not a great *Hamlet, or a* deep *Hamlet, but he doesn't fall on his face."*
—NEWSWEEK, 12/31/90

"Never less than forthright and well spoken, Gibson's performance, once it gets going, is also witty, intelligent, and full of emotional surprises. Of the 30-odd Hamlets I've seen, his is certainly the most straight-talking."
—VILLAGE VOICE, 1/1/91

"He [Gibson] reads the speeches very simply, with

Hamlet accuses his mother (Glenn Close) of adultery—and worse—in an Oedipal confrontation that almost borders on sexual assault.

great intensity; he is always intelligible and sometimes moving, but nothing in the performance soars, and his temperamental range is much too narrow."

—*NEW YORK*, 1/21/91

"For the most part, Gibson's performance is excessively august, as if he were trying above all to live down the flightier connotations of his usual image."

—*SIGHT AND SOUND*, 5/91

Franco Zeffirelli's lusty reimagining of Shakespeare's *Hamlet* for the 1990s is one of the most exciting—and accessible—film versions of the classic play ever made. And Mel Gibson takes to the title role as if to the manor born.

As envisioned by Zeffirelli, the character of Hamlet has so much in common with other characters Gibson has played throughout his career that the star's decision to finally take a stab at the role seems more of an inevitability than the bold and unexpected actor's "stunt" many critics assessed it as being. In many ways, the character is the archetype of Gibson's screen persona.

In a thoughtful commentary written for the film's press kit, Shakespearean scholar Prof. Frank Kermode says of Hamlet: "He has the arrogance and charm and sometimes the courtesy of a prince, as well as the moodiness and

The desperate Hamlet swears Horatio to silence about seeing the ghost of his father so he can plot his revenge against the monarch's killers.

146

147

occasionally the craziness of a clever student. He is vivid, dangerous, unpredictable, violent, crazy even when he's not pretending to be."

In varying ways, this description fits Gibson's Frank Dunne in *Gallipoli,* Guy Hamilton in *The Year of Living Dangerously,* Fletcher Christian in *The Bounty,* and of course, Martin Riggs in *Lethal Weapon.* It can be applied in some measure to many other characters Gibson has played in the movies as well.

In Shakespeare's text, the vengeful prince of Denmark broods: "The time is out of joint: | O cursed spite, | That ever I was born to set it right!" and "now could I drink hot blood, | And do such bitter business as the day | Would quake to look on." He could be speaking for Mad Max and *Braveheart*'s William Wallace also.

Add to this Zeffirelli's own assessment of Hamlet as a man of vitality who is "often very trenchant and funny, knows basically that he's not born to be king—he's born to be something else, but what that is he doesn't know—and who is torn by his desire to act and by his difficulty in deciding what to do and when to do it" and it's easy to see why the adapter-director thought Gibson was "exactly right for the role."

It's also easy to see why Gibson responded so enthusiastically, for *Hamlet* was not the anomaly in his career it appeared to be to his astonished and sometimes dismissive critics. The themes of the play and the nuances of the character are ones Gibson had been exploring on-screen in one form or another his entire professional life—and would continue to, both in personal projects like *Braveheart* and in commercial endeavors like *Ransom.* The part also presented Gibson with the ultimate challenge in sustaining the audience's allegiance and affection because Hamlet is not only a vacillating hero but, indeed, a destructive and often alienating one.

Perhaps anticipating the inevitable, if pointless, comparisons between his performance in the role and other famous Hamlets of stage and screen, Gibson interestingly chose to play many of the character's most famous set pieces, such as the "To be or not to be" soliloquy, in a low key, then rip into other less well known scenes with an unanticipated gusto, making the part all his own.

A good example is Hamlet's confrontation with Rosencrantz (Michael Maloney) and

Guildenstern (Sean Murray), two old friends now sent to spy on him by the villainous usurper King Claudius (Alan Bates). Attuned to their deceit, he challenges one of the spies to play the flute. Not knowing how, the fellow declines, and Hamlet subjects the knave to a withering rebuke for believing he, Hamlet, can be "played" (i.e., toyed with or manipulated) easier than a flute. Gibson's unexpected explosion at his character's being insulted like this reveals another facet of Hamlet seldom explored: the man may be hobbled by indeci-

His faith in women destroyed by his mother, Hamlet rebukes and rebuffs Ophelia (Helena Bonham-Carter), the woman he loves most and who loves him.

sion, but he has a sizable ego nonetheless.

Gibson keeps surprising us like this throughout the film, bringing fireworks to scenes which previous screen versions of the play often lacked or additional fireworks to other scenes that already have them, such as the one where he accuses his mother, Queen Gertrude (Glenn Close), of infidelity and complicity in his father's murder. He transforms the scene into a supercharged Oedipal confrontation that borders on sexual assault as he shockingly simulates intercourse, vilifying her in his grief and disgust for being nothing more than a common whore and adding a disturbing meaning to his disaffected character's "frailty thy name is woman" recriminations that we've seldom seen before and an emotional sting we've never felt.

Glenn Close, who admitted to being as startled by Gibson's acting choice here as we are, is shatteringly believable in her terrified response to Hamlet's behavior and accusations in this scene. She turns the relatively shallow character of Queen Gertude, who is doomed by her girlish adoration of Claudius and inability to believe his crime (which she took no part in), into a three-dimensional, and ultimately tragic, human being, making the part very much *her* own. She's superb in the film, as is the entire cast.

Apart from Gibson's performance (he's not just a good Hamlet; he's an *excellent* one), what makes this *Hamlet* a triumph is that it works so well as a movie. It has real suspense, even though every twist and turn of the plot is universally so well known. "Movies can tell so much in one shot that even Shakespeare's words become redundant," Zeffirelli says of his adaptation. "My efforts were to keep the story clear without mutilating the original. We made some tough choices, and some of them may be controversial. But it is the eye of the camera

150

that makes the difference."

Among these controversial choices was telescoping so much more into the play-within-a-play scene than other directors have done. In the scene, Hamlet has a visiting theatrical troupe stage a re-creation of his father's murder as that night's entertainment in order to expose Gertrude and Claudius's crimes. By substituting much of Shakespeare's text with wordless reaction shots between the accuser and the accused as the surrogate drama unfolds and increasing the momentum of these shots, Zeffirelli creates what Professor Kermode describes as an "atmosphere of diseased excitement" that builds to an explosive climax with a tension that is almost palpable—as if Hitchcock were doing Shakespeare.

Boldly, Zeffirelli also transposes Hamlet's famous "get thee to a nunnery" scene with Ophelia, located elsewhere in the play, to the play-within-a-play scene, where it not only fits more powerfully but works more heartbreakingly.

Often a thankless role in other film versions, the doomed Ophelia is not so here. Helena Bonham Carter's performance as the young woman whom Hamlet drives mad and destroys by withdrawing his love (and killing her father) is as powerfully reimagined as Gibson's Hamlet and the play itself in this remarkable movie.

"I am dead." Hamlet, mortally wounded by Laertes, faces the end over the corpse of his mother, the victim of a lethal dose of poison meant for Hamlet himself.

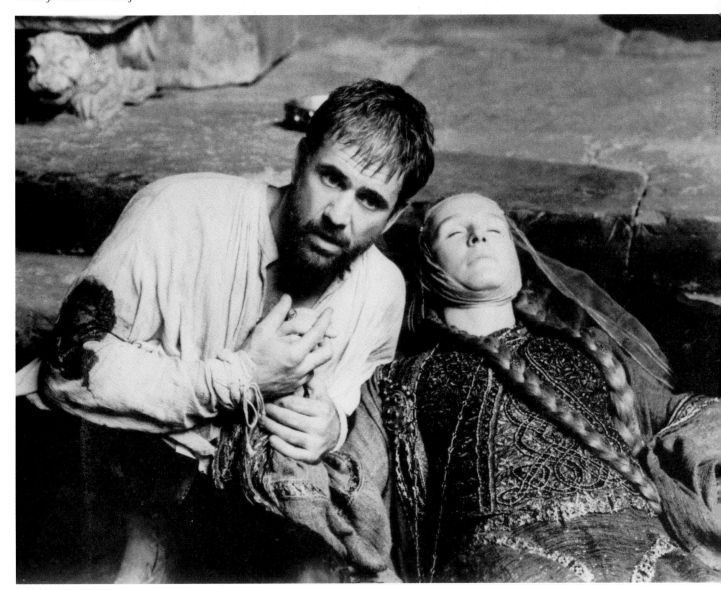

FOREVER YOUNG

1992—WARNER BROS.

"I wanted to make one I could take the kids to."

—MEL GIBSON

18

CREDITS
Producer: Bruce Davey; *Director:* Steve Miner; *Screenwriter:* Jeffrey Abrams; *Cinematographer:* Russell Boyd; *Editor:* Jon Poll; *Composer:* Jerry Goldsmith; *Production designer:* Gregg Fonseca.
Running time: 102 minutes.

CAST
Mel Gibson *(Daniel);* Jamie Lee Curtis *(Claire);* Elijah Wood *(Nat);* Isabel Glasser *(Helen);* George Wendt *(Harry);* Joe Morton *(Cameron);* Nicholas Surovy *(John);* David Marshall Grant *(Wilcox);* Robert Hy Gorman *(Felix);* Millie Slavin *(Susan Finley);* Michael Goorjian *(Steven);* Veronica Lauren *(Alice);* Art LaFleur *(Alice's Father);* Eric Pierpont *(Fred);* Walt Goggins *(Gate MP).*

REVIEWS

"Gibson is such a disarming actor that he actually makes this big-kid fantasia vaguely watchable."
—LOS ANGELES TIMES, 12/16/92

"Gibson himself is generally convincing, and sweet, although it's a particularly humorless role. Although he's thrust into a comical situation, he never seems to get the joke himself."
—NEWSDAY, 12/16/92

"Gibson's baffled hero act is beginning to lose its charm."
—NEWSWEEK, 12/28/92

Forever Young is the story of an Army Air Corps test pilot (Gibson) who can't summon the nerve to tell his childhood sweetheart, Helen (Isabel Glasser) he loves her and ask her to marry him. Moments after his latest attack of being tongue-tied, she's acci-

Daniel (Mel Gibson) can't summon the nerve to tell his childhood sweetheart Helen (Isabel Glasser) that he loves her. Soon it will be too late.

154

LETHAL WEAPON 3

1992—WARNER BROS.

"There's an interesting reversal of roles in this one, because something happens to Murtaugh, and Riggs is called upon to pull him out of a deep emotional tailspin, much the way Murtaugh had to help Riggs in the original. In a way, it's an exploration of what all friends do for each other—but on a grand scale!"

—MEL GIBSON

CREDITS

Producers: Richard Donner and Joel Silver; *Director:* Richard Donner; *Screenwriters:* Jeffrey Boam and Robert Mark Kamen, from a story by Boam based on characters created by Shane Black; *Cinematographer:* Jan De Bont; *Editors:* Robert Brown and Battle Davis; *Composers:* Michael Kamen, Eric Clapton, and David Sanborn; *Production designer:* James Spencer. Running time: 118 minutes.

CAST

Mel Gibson *(Martin Riggs);* Danny Glover *(Roger Murtaugh);* Joe Pesci *(Leo Getz);* René Russo *(Lorna Cole);* Stuart Wilson *(Jack Travis);* Steve Kahan *(Captain Murphy);* Darlene Love *(Trish Murtaugh);* Traci Wolfe *(Rianne Murtaugh);* Damon Hines *(Nick Murtaugh);* Ebonie Smith *(Carrie Murtaugh);* Gregory Millar *(Tyrone);* Nick Chinlund *(Hatchett);* Jason Meshover-Iorg *(Young Cop);* Alan Scarfe *(Herman Walters);* Delores Hall *(Delores).*

REVIEWS

"Gibson and Glover have turned their duet into a soft-shoe routine with firepower."

—LOS ANGELES TIMES, 5/15/92

"Gibson and Glover, at home in their roles, apply an expertly light touch; they don't take this stuff seriously, but they don't act like they're above it either."

—NEW YORK POST, 5/15/92

"The gleam in Gibson's eye is beginning to look fatuous. Throwing himself around like a kid, he races through his lines, jabbering right across the other actors. He's becoming a hog and a clown, a mass of hyperactive reflexes and 'charm' without meaning."

—NEW YORK, 6/1/92

Internal Affairs investigator Lorna Cole (René Russo) teams with Riggs (Gibson) and Murtaugh (Danny Glover) to bring down a crooked cop.

Glover, Joe Pesci, and Gibson—the Larry, Curly, and Moe of the action-thriller genre—reunite for Lethal Weapon 3.

Like *Mad Max Beyond Thunderdome, Lethal Weapon 3* is one movie too many in the series insofar as offering us anything new is concerned. Although the film is bigger and noisier than its predecessors, the formula has begun to show, and the result is routine.

All the ingredients that made the first two *Lethal Weapon* films wildly popular are back: the banter between the two cop buddies ("I'm too old for this shit, Riggs." "Aren't you going to miss all this when you retire, Rog?"); the outrageous puns; the salutes to the Three Stooges; the nonstop action and thrills; even Joe Pesci's character Leo Getz, who is now a Beverly Hills real estate agent, though he's lost none of his knack for getting in Riggs and Murtaugh's way at critical times.

But here the ingredients generate exhaustion rather than laughs. Like Pesci's character, who is more annoying than amusing and who conveniently disappears for large chunks of the

film because there's not a lot for him to do, the movie wears us out trying to ratchet up the excitement while covering the same old ground.

The picture opens with a bang as Riggs and Murtaugh stumble upon an office building where a bomb has been planted. The device has enough explosive power to level the eight-story structure in seconds.

With just seven days to go before retirement, Murtaugh wants to play it safe and wait for the bomb squad that helped him through his toilet-seat adventure in the previous film. But the daredevil Riggs is all for trying to defuse the bomb and proceeds to cut the wires. He snips the wrong wire, however; running for their lives, they get out just in time. The bomb detonates, and the entire building explodes around them.

This amazing sequence, the most spectacular in the series, was shot in Florida, where

160

With just seven days to go before retirement, Murtaugh (Danny Glover) is demoted from detective to patrolman along with Riggs (Mel Gibson) because of his partner's rule-breaking ways.

producer Joel Silver was invited to film the demolition of an actual building, Orlando's old city hall. To create the illusion of a bomb blast rather than a straightforward demolition, special-effects supervisor Matt Sweeney rigged the building with gallon drums of debris and powder that exploded four-thousand pounds of glass, cork, and paper from the windows on cue.

Having survived this job by the skin of their teeth, Riggs and Murtaugh return to their current assignment of investigating the theft of illegal weapons slated for destruction from a police lockup; the weapons have been turning up on the streets in the hands of youth gangs.

Their chief suspect is an ex-cop gone bad whom detective Lorna Cole (René Russo), in the department's Internal Affairs Division, has also been investigating. A fast-talking, hard-driving, mean-fighting cop with nerves of steel (Riggs's female alter ego, in other words), Cole is determined to nail the bad guy on her own

and refuses to share her information. Infuriated, Riggs disparages her with one of his puns, calling her "Infernal Repairs," their mutual antagonism mirroring the early relationship between Riggs and Murtaugh in the first film.

Soon their antagonism turns to love, however, as they realize how much they have in common. In fact, she uses a screen saver bearing the faces of The Three Stooges on her home computer monitor. Is she the gal for Riggs, or what!

The gradual awareness of their attraction to each other leads to an amusing love scene, which escalates from one-upsmanship to foreplay, in which they strip, comparing their respective scars from wounds suffered on the job.

Meanwhile, Murtaugh, now just a few days from retirement, is forced to shoot an armed gang member in self-defense and goes into an emotional tailspin.

The rationale for his crisis of conscience—the victim was a teenager and a close friend of Murtaugh's son—is a stretch, for, between them, Murtaugh and Riggs have slain hundreds of people in the series already without batting an eye.

Nevertheless, Murtaugh's breakdown sets up a scene between the cop buddies that approaches the acting highs of the first film and strikes the emotional chord of the toilet-bomb sequence in *Lethal Weapon 2* as Riggs tries to ease his drunken friend's conscience by convincing him he had no choice in the shooting. Murtaugh not only spurns Riggs's counsel but rebukes Riggs for getting him involved in so much violence in the first place. All he wants now is to retire and be left alone.

Riggs gets drunk, too, as they engage in an emotional shouting match in which Riggs reveals his insecurities about Murtaugh's retirement and accuses his friend of giving no thought to its impact on his younger partner, for the two share a closer relationship than most married couples. Riggs's outpouring brings Murtaugh up short as he realizes the emotional truth of it for him as well. He needs Riggs as much as Riggs needs him.

The housing tract goes up in flames in the spectacular finale as Riggs once again proves himself to be the LAPD's most lethal weapon.

Without each other, each will be less than what they are together.

This powerfully performed scene is the high point of the movie because it brings the otherwise wildly cartoonish *Lethal Weapon 3* down to earth for a few moments of needed refocusing on what the movie—and the series—is all about: the relationship between Riggs and Murtaugh, not the pyrotechnics which surround and, in this installment, engulf that relationship.

After that, *Lethal Weapon 3* gets back on the shtick, culminating in a gigantic shoot-out at a housing development into which the bad guy has been funneling his profits from the sale of

the stolen weapons.

Like the building we saw demolished at the beginning of the film, this location was real—an abandoned housing tract that fell victim to the S&L fiasco, sat unfinished for several years, and was scheduled for destruction. Once again, the special-effects crew stepped in to help, and the entire fifty-six houses in the abandoned tract were torched, leveled, then bulldozed for the film's fiery, explosion-filled finale.

Except that it isn't *the* fiery, explosion-filled finale. Keep watching after the closing credits and you'll see what I mean.

163

THE MAN WITHOUT A FACE

1993—WARNER BROS.

"In my business, we're always judged on appearances first. I wanted to make a statement against that."

—MEL GIBSON

CREDITS

Producer: Bruce Davey; *Director:* Mel Gibson; *Screenwriter:* Malcolm MacRury, based on the novel by Isabelle Holland; *Cinematographer:* Donald McAlpine; *Editor:* Tony Gibbs; *Composer:* James Horner; *Production designer:* Barbara Dunphy.
Running time: 114 minutes.

CAST

Mel Gibson *(Justin McLeod);* Margaret Whitton *(Catherine);* Fay Masterson *(Gloria);* Gaby Hoffman *(Megan);* Geoffrey Lewis *(Chief Stark);* Richard Masur *(Carl);* Nick Stahl *(Chuck);* Michael De Luise *(Douglas Hall);* Ethan Phillips *(Mr. Lansing);* Jean De Baer *(Mrs. Lansing);* Jack De Mave *(Mr. Cooper);* Viva *(Mrs. Cooper);* Justin Kanew *(Rob Lansing);* Sean Kellman *(David Taylor-Fife);* Chris Lineburg *(Scott Pearson).*

REVIEWS

"Gibson the actor . . . wears his astonishing make-up with total conviction, never once resorting to the melodramatic excesses that must have been such a powerful temptation in this unusual role."

—NEW YORK POST, 8/25/93

"Mel Gibson, directing for the first time, presents this deeply wet material in a remarkably cool and dry manner. But his film is in desperate need of smarm busting—something, anything that would relieve the familiarity of its characters, the predictability of its structure, the bland failure to challenge its perfect correctness of outlook."

—TIME, 8/30/93

"The Man Without a Face is such a noble, well-intentioned film—a cross between Dead Poet's Society *and* The Phantom of the Opera *done as an after-school special—that one feels like an ogre picking on it. As a director, Gibson's strongest suit is his work with the actors—particularly his young star Stahl, a natural who possesses great emotional range. If the whole project had Stahl's honesty, it might have been the little gem it so earnestly means to be."*

—NEWSWEEK, 8/30/93

Gibson's McLeod is another of the actor's flawed heroes, a man able to help others achieve what he cannot fully achieve himself.

Mel Gibson directs Nick Stahl as Chuck in the coming-of-age drama The Man Without a Face.

"Mel Gibson's The Man Without a Face *is more interesting than it has a right to be, and far more strange than it knows. Given Mel's macho reputation on screen and off, the film's moralism is to put it mildly, a wee overdetermined. Furiously intent on celebrating male love (chaste, pure, honorable), Gibson and company try to refuse the erotics of friendship, and miserably, wonderously, fail."*

—VILLAGE VOICE, 8/31/93

The ingratiating bewilderment and poignancy he brought to his character in *Forever Young* marked the first time in more than twelve films as a superstar that Mel Gibson patently recalled his performance as the childlike Tim in a big-budget feature. Interestingly, the vehicle he chose for his directorial debut shortly thereafter, *The Man Without a Face*, harkens back to the same film.

A superstar with his own production company and possessing a yen to direct, Gibson could probably have selected any subject he wanted for his debut behind the camera. That

As Justin McLeod, a mysterious recluse with a past who befriends a troubled young boy.

he selected not an action movie, the genre with which he is most associated, but a subject much like *Tim* in both story and theme is indicative of *Tim*'s importance in his filmography and the place it must hold in his heart.

There are differences between the two films, of course, but the similarities are striking. To this author's knowledge, Gibson has not commented on these similarities in any published interviews about *The Man Without a Face*. In fact, he has publicly said little about the project's genesis. "We found it in Nova Scotia," he told an interviewer for the Director's Guild of America's membership magazine—"it" being a script based on Isabelle Holland's novel by Canadian television writer Malcolm MacRury, who was seeking to make his debut as a writer of features. But the similarities with *Tim* exist and may have been what drew him to the project.

Both are dramas about overcoming loneliness, learning to become an adult, and a relationship built on understanding, companionship, and tolerance that is condemned by others but which transforms the protagonists' lives.

However, in *The Man Without a Face* the relationship doesn't have a sexual element—

though society misjudges it as having one—and the roles are reversed. Here it is Mel Gibson who plays the Piper Laurie part and Nick Stahl the role of Tim, an actual boy not a boy-man in this case, and also not retarded, although he is perceived as not being all that bright and is taunted by his siblings as weird and stupid.

By responding to the boy's searching questions on life, death, and other weighty, adult matters which his mother and others have had no time for or felt the boy wouldn't understand, Gibson helps Stahl mature emotionally, just as Piper Laurie did with Gibson in the earlier film. And, like Laurie, the responsibility for the boy that Gibson's character in *Face* at first hesitantly undertakes ultimately has an emotionally healing effect on him, too.

In the course of things, Gibson's character in *Face* is also revealed to be yet another of the actor's flawed heroes, the man who is able to help others achieve what he cannot fully achieve himself—a lineage going all the way back to the *Mad Max* series and leading directly into his next project behind the camera, *Braveheart*.

And while Gibson may have the title role here, he disappears into it as if it were a character part—which he reinforces by concealing his looks behind the character's fire-scarred makeup—and lets young Stahl be the leading man, making *The Man Without a Face* "a Mel Gibson Film" in every respect.

The film is a memoir narrated in flashback by its young protagonist, Chuck Norstadt (Stahl), who picks up his tale several years earlier, when he was summering in Maine with his much-married mother (now seeking husband number five) and two resentful half sisters. The atmosphere of his home life is mightily dysfunctional; he feels like an outsider in his own family and is desperately unhappy. He seeks to escape and find his own place in the world by following in the footsteps of his late father, who disappeared from the boy's life early on and about whom Chuck knows very little other than that the man, a test pilot, died in a plane crash.

He has put his father on a private pedestal.

Chuck wants to spend the summer boning up for an entrance exam to his father's alma mater. Having failed the exam once, his efforts to try again are greeted with skepticism and a

lack of support from his mother and taunts from his sisters. He resolves to find the help and support he needs from an outside source and connects with another outsider, a disfigured former prep-school teacher named McLeod, who now lives as a recluse in an old, dark house overlooking the sea, shunning society like a character in a horror movie.

The victim of a car crash that claimed the life of a student in the car with him, the hideously scarred McLeod has never considered plastic surgery, electing instead to wear his disfigurement as a badge of self-flagellating dishonor—and guilt—for the incident, which cost him his teaching career due to the whispered rumors of sexual misconduct surrounding it. He also uses the disfigurement as a weapon to keep the world at bay.

Frightened by the "monster" at first, then intimidated by McLeod's brusque manner, Chuck nevertheless persists in winning McLeod over. Their student-teacher relationship turns to friendship as they share thoughts and feelings and learn from each other. Chuck gains confidence in his intellectual abilities and realizes he's not stupid, after all; he's just never before had his eyes opened to learning by a teacher as gifted as McLeod. McLeod rediscovers the joy of teaching again as well as the ability to relate to another human being.

When, during an argument with his older half sister Gloria (Fay Masterson), Chuck is viciously told the truth about his father (an alcoholic who abused his wife and family when drunk and committed suicide in an asylum), the boy is emotionally devastated, his idol destroyed, and turns to the only one he feels will understand, his friend McLeod, who gives him shelter for the night. But when the sheriff (Geoffrey Lewis) finds the boy there the next morning, he suspects the worst because of the rumors surrounding McLeod's past history, and hysteria sweeps the community when word gets out that McLeod has been "tutoring" the boy all summer long. Chuck's mother, Catherine (Margaret Whitton), becomes McLeod's chief accuser, and the man is ordered to stay away from the boy or charges of sexual abuse will be brought against him. Chuck's idolatry of McLeod is shattered by the allegations the man was having an affair with the boy who died in the car crash; he demands the truth from his friend. But as McLeod points out, Chuck already knows the truth, as do we, that the accusations, past *and* present, are untrue. Nevertheless, he must say goodbye to his mentor forever. But he successfully passes the exam and is on his way to adulthood.

Chuck sees his friend and mentor just one more time—at graduation some years later. McLeod appears at the edge of the crowd to give Chuck a victory salute, then disappears from the boy's life, but not his memory, forever.

As for McLeod, he is seen only in long shot at the end, his face shaded by sunglasses. But there is a suggestion that his face is no longer disfigured, that in the intervening years he got the plastic surgery he'd long denied himself and has finally made peace with himself and the world because of what the friendship with Chuck taught him.

Like many films about troubled youth, *The Man Without a Face* tends to overexaggerate the insensitivity and thick-headedness of its adult characters (McLeod excluded), reducing them to types: the self-absorbed mom, the cop just doing his duty, the uncaring bureaucrat, and so on. They're set up as straw figures to be knocked down so that our sympathy for and identification with Chuck and McLeod will be enhanced. As often happens when the balance is tipped so one-sidedly, credibility suffers, and the emotional force of the drama is weakened.

The film is also a bit too loaded with incident. Putting it another way, the script includes so many deep, dark secrets about the characters' pasts that after a while the revelations start to feel contrived. A good example is the issue of sexual misconduct. Apart from reinforcing another link with *Tim* and contriving a convenient motive for the separation of student and teacher at the end (which itself is unnecessary to the story), it serves no function except to add another plot twist. Some critics felt Gibson should have dealt with this issue—derived from the novel—more boldly. On the contrary, I feel it should have been dispensed with altogether as melodramatic overkill.

Wisely, director Gibson focuses most of the film's attention on the evolving friendship between McLeod and Chuck (Stahl, a real find, is wonderful in the role); it, after all, is the crux of the story and the emotional core of the film. The warmth and believability of their relationship, which is not always harmonious even after they become friends, are what give *The Man Without a Face* what *Tim* had: heart.

A gifted and demanding teacher, McLeod helps Chuck gain intellectual confidence, and the two become close friends.

MAVERICK

1994—WARNER BROS.

"It's not a bona fide western. It's a send-up."

—MEL GIBSON

CREDITS

Producers: Richard Donner and Bruce Davey; *Director:* Richard Donner; *Screenwriter:* William Goldman; *Cinematographer:* Vilmos Zsigmond; *Editors:* Stuart Baird and Mike Kelly; *Composer:* Randy Newman; *Production designer:* Tom Sanders.
Running time: 129 minutes.

CAST

Mel Gibson *(Bret Maverick);* Jodie Foster *(Annabelle Bransford);* James Garner *(Zane Cooper);* Graham Greene *(Joseph);* Alfred Molina *(Angel);* James Coburn *(Commodore);* Dub Taylor *(Room Clerk);* Geoffrey Lewis *(Matthew Wicker);* Paul L. Smith *(Archduke);* Dan Hedaya *(Twitchy);* Dennis Fimple *(Stuttering);* Denver Pyle *(Old Gambler);* Clint Black *(Sweet-faced Gambler);* Max Perlich *(Johnny Hardin);* Jean De Baer *(Margret Mary);* Vince Gill, Janice Gill, William Smith, Doug McClure, Henry Darrow, Robert Fuller, William Marshal *(Cameo appearances).*

REVIEWS

"The title role provides Gibson with a cocky, physical character that suits his persona. Unlike his TV pre-

decessor, he loves to fight as much as he likes to banter."

—VARIETY, 5/16/94

"Mr. Gibson, one of our best comic actors, plays Maverick with a gleam in his eye, knowing enough not to take the character too seriously."

—NEW YORK TIMES, 5/20/94

"The new Bret Maverick is a different kind of charmer: an antsy, wild-eyed, motormouthed one, who, not surprisingly, bears more than a passing resemblance to the deranged daredevil cop that Gibson plays in the mega-grossing Lethal Weapon *movies."*

—NEW YORKER, 6/6/94

"Taking the old James Garner role, Gibson, running around bare-chested, is lithe and powerful, a far more physical performer than the hyper-relaxed Garner, who preferred acting with his voice and smile. A cardsharp and wit, a daredevil clown and acrobat, this Maverick can beat you a dozen ways."

—NEW YORK, 6/6/94

Maverick (Mel Gibson) may prefer living by his wits but can get physical when he has to. Here, he stops a runaway stagecoach as passengers Foster and Garner hang on.

Back in the late 1950s, when the western was still riding high on television and at the movies, along came the classic TV series *Maverick* to poke fun at the genre's well-worn conventions, making them difficult to accept with a straight face from then on. Within a decade, the classic horse opera was all but dead in popularity and esteem.

More than a generation later, just as the western was attempting one of its periodic comebacks on the big screen, along came this new, big screen *Maverick* to dig another grave for the genre even faster. Barely had Kevin Costner's paean to the American Indian, *Dances With Wolves* (1990), gotten audiences to take the stock western movie character of the noble savage seriously again when up popped authentic Indian actor Graham Greene to lampoon

Spoofing every cliché of the movie western imaginable, Maverick *takes dead aim and shoots the genre right between the eyes. The genre's comeback never had a chance.*

that character in *Maverick*—a character Greene himself had played absolutely straight in *Wolves.*

Speaking in a Native American language cooked up between them to con the white-eyed suckers—a sort of patois of gibberish amusingly translated for us in subtitles—he and his pal Maverick (whom he calls "Mav") conspire to get Greene's tribe to mount a hostile attack for show so that Mav can emerge the hero and the Indians can make a few bucks. So much for the cliché of the noble savage; like many other conventions of the western, particularly the modern, revisionist kind, *Maverick* takes dead aim and shoots it right between the eyes. The genre's comeback never had a chance.

There are some major differences between the TV *Maverick* and the movie version, however. Working within a tight, hour-long format, the TV show kept its plots lean and directed its sly barbs with a leisurely aim. Weighing in at more than two hours, the movie version has enough plot twists to fill a dozen episodes of the TV series.

Essentially, the film is about Maverick's attempts to come up with the remaining three-thousand dollars he needs to pay his entrance fee to a high-stakes poker game—the mother of all such games, in fact. A championship tournament of cardsharps, the game is set to take place on a steamboat, a sort of floating Las Vegas.

How he gets the money, only to keep losing and getting it back again, constitutes the main plot, but there are countless other subplots, too. They involve his on-again, off-again relationship with a lady cardsharp, Annabelle Bransford (played by Jodie Foster), who wants to get into his pockets as well as his pants, numerous run-ins with bad guy Angel (Alfred

Mel Gibson stares down a sore loser in Maverick. *The movie has enough plot twists to fill a dozen episodes of the classic TV series that inspired it.*

Maverick (Gibson) teams up with a lady cardsharp (Jodie Foster) and a shady lawman (James Garner), encountering numerous adventures along the way to a high-stakes poker game.

Molina)—a sore loser who is hot on the gambler's trail—and connection to a shady lawman, Zane Cooper (played by James Garner), who's also pretty good at cards.

The TV show went for the mischievous wink, but the movie version goes for the big joke on a broad scale—and feels the need to keep jabbing us in the ribs to see if we get it.

One of the jokes (as in the series) centers on Maverick's cowardice, his preference for relying on his wits rather than gunplay and brawn to ensure his longevity in the Wild West. Heroes, especially in westerns, can't *really* be cowards, of course. But the cheekiness of the TV show was that Bret Maverick, as played by James Garner, was precisely what he preached. Though fast on the draw, he slyly wiggled out of every confrontation that might force him to prove it.

In the movie, Gibson shares the same phi-losophy, one which he expresses in almost the first scene when he's accused of cheating at cards by gunslinger John Wesley Hardin (played by Max Perlich) and told to "reach for it." Declining the opportunity to go up against a professional gunman and saying with a shrug, "Yes, I guess so," at the suggestion that he's a coward, Mel's Maverick then proceeds to wow Hardin—and us—by drawing his gun faster than the eye can blink.

It's a funny gag, but the filmmakers can't leave it alone; they have Gibson engage in some extravagant *Lethal Weapon*-style twirls, tosses, and other bravado tricks with the gun to make his adversary back down all the more. Even worse than bludgeoning what was a good joke to death, this undercuts the spirit of the original series, which the film had so far retained, by making mincemeat of what makes the character Maverick. Here Gibson's Maverick may *say* he wishes to avoid confrontation, but when it occurs, he can't stop showing off how good he is.

Shortly thereafter, Gibson is threatened by some other rowdies, who believe he's cheated them; outnumbered, he faces a beating. After doing the "Yes, I guess I'm a coward" routine *again*—this time he removes his coat so it won't get ruined—he decimates the bunch without so much as mussing a hair, then shows off some more. Same joke, same payoff, same point.

There are some big laughs in *Maverick*, but the filmmakers' heavy-handed approach of relentlessly repeating each joke throughout the movie as if not trusting us to have gotten it the first time is wearing. It makes the film seem longer than it needs to be—because it is—and dilutes the fun.

Only James Garner's dry performance as the shady lawman is consistently on the mark and in tune with the original. In fact, he turns out to be the film's *real* Maverick in more ways than one. As for Jodie Foster, she's not often called upon to be frilly and feminine in her film roles, but such qualities are her only requirements here, and she fulfills her obligations nicely, even throwing "funny" and "cute" into her change-of-pace role.

Backed up by Cooper (Garner), Maverick proves himself no coward when it comes to handling a gun.

BRAVEHEART

1995—PARAMOUNT PICTURES

"I love it. All that hard labor paid off."
—MEL GIBSON

CREDITS

Producers: Mel Gibson, Alan Ladd Jr., and Bruce Davey;
Director: Mel Gibson; *Screenwriter:* Randall Wallace;
Cinematographer: John Toll; *Editors:* Steve Rosenblum and
Victor Dubois; *Music:* James Horner; *Production designer:*
Tom Sanders.
Running time: 178 minutes.

CAST

Mel Gibson *(William Wallace)*; Sophie Marceau *(Princess
Isabelle)*; Patrick McGoohan *(Longshanks—King Edward I)*;
Catherine McCormack *(Murron)*; Angus Macfadyen
(Robert the Bruce); Brendan Gleeson *(Hamish)*; David
O'Hara *(Stephen)*; Ian Bannen *(Leper)*; James Robinson
(Young William); Sean Lawlor *(Malcolm Wallace)*; Sandy
Nelson *(John Wallace)*; James Cosmo *(Campbell)*; Sean
McGinley *(MacClannough)*; Alal Tall *(Elder Stewart)*;
Andrew Weir *(Young Hamish)*; Brian Cox *(Argyle Wallace)*;
Donal Gibson *(Stewart)*.

REVIEWS

*"Gibson has little to learn about showcasing his
own charisma. As William, he's an enticing mixture
of sinewy heroics and studly blue-eyed dazzle."*
—ENTERTAINMENT WEEKLY, 5/26/95

*"Braveheart runs almost three hours, and though
it's full of incident, including several big and
expertly staged battle sequences, it really doesn't have
enough on its mind to sustain our full attention
over that span."*
—TIME, 5/29/95

*"An impressive achievement, Gibson's honorable
shot at a big, resonant paean to freedom, like Spartacus. But it's too long at nearly three hours; there's
too much repeating of treacheries and battles."*
—NEWSWEEK, 5/29/95

*"The love scenes are so-so, the political scenes ho-
hum, but the fighting—both individual contests
and mass battle scenes—is first-rate, barbaric and
sublime."*
—NATIONAL REVIEW, 6/10/95

*Wallace allows his hatred of his enemies and savage thirst for
their blood overtake and ultimately doom him—a grave miscalculation the cooler and less passionate Mad Max would never
have made.*

There's a moment early in *Braveheart* when Gibson's William Wallace, having slain several British soldiers in reprisal for the murder of his wife, finds himself cornered in a small village and outnumbered.

As the soldiers go from hut to hut searching for him, he overcomes a soldier inside one of these huts and dons the man's uniform. He joins the searchers with a friendly wave, then makes an abrupt turn when their backs are to him and scurries away to freedom, fairly tripping on the ill-fitting clothes.

The pantomimed scene is staged like a

slapstick routine from an old Buster Keaton comedy, but rather than striking a false note, it caps off the grim proceedings with a leavening laugh. An aficionado of slapstick and longtime admirer of Keaton's films, which director George Miller introduced him to while they were making the *Mad Max* movies, Gibson seems to be saying that even the direst events have their funny moments or life wouldn't be worth living—and freedom wouldn't be worth dying for—in the first place.

This is quintessential Mel Gibson, who is well known for breaking the tension on-screen

With Catherine McCormack as Murron. Childhood sweethearts, they are married in secret to avoid the law of prima nocte. *Her murder motivates his revenge, like Mad Max's.*

and off with sudden displays of outrageous and seemingly inappropriate bursts of humor. That he would dare to do the same here shows how personal and self-revelatory a project *Braveheart* was for him. It is also a wonderful directorial touch that not only encapsulates the epic film's theme cinematically but does so in a style a less involved or less self-confident filmmaker might not think of or risk.

There are moments like this sprinkled throughout *Braveheart*, a film widely heralded for its breathtaking and ultraviolent battle scenes, but not for the audaciousness of its craft. Mel Gibson took a lot of chances with this film, an obvious labor of love. By turns sentimental, romantic, philosophical, zany, and rip-roaringly action filled, it virtually invited critics to dismiss it as "*Mad Max* in a kilt"—or "Mad Mac" as Gibson self-deprecatingly predicted prior to the film's opening. Instead it won people's hearts and the Oscar—an award usually geared to box office but sometimes bestowed for courage, as may have been the case here.

Among other things, Mel Gibson was inspired to make *Braveheart* because of the epic films he was thrilled by as a youth. He places Stanley Kubrick's *Spartacus* high on the list of *Braveheart's* influences. In fact, *Braveheart* is *Spartacus*.

Both films deal with a real figure about whom history knows little. Only the basic facts survive about their respective struggles for freedom against their tyrannical foreign oppressors—Rome in Spartacus's case, England in William Wallace's—a struggle each man went to his death failing to win. The rest is myth. Both films surround that myth with as much known historical detail as possible to flesh out their larger-than-life central characters and make them real.

A Greek slave trained as a gladiator for the sport of his Roman masters, Spartacus rebels due to the subhuman treatment of his class. A peace-loving Scottish farmer's lad whose family was deceived and then killed by the English, William Wallace finally rebels when England's ruthless British king Edward I reinstates the law of *prima nocte* to keep the English bloodline flowing throughout Scotland and maintain his hold on the country. The law gives the local English magistrates first dibs on any new bride on her wedding night. Wallace marries his childhood sweetheart, Murron, in secret to keep her from the law. When the magistrate finds out, he and his men come after Wallace; to flush him out into the open, they slit Murron's throat in the public square.

Flush him out this does. In a vengeful

181

Wallace vows to bring England to its knees and free Scotland.

bloodbath, Wallace kills all but one of the murderers, then sends the survivor to the English king with a message, that from here on Scotland is free. Wallace spends the rest of the film battling against the British with brutal and uncompromising fierceness to make that promise come true. In the end, he is deceived by a clique of Scottish nobles, who prefer the comfortable status quo to the uncertainty of freedom, and by the English, who want to make an example of the upstart rebel. Captured and tortured to death for his heresy, Wallace goes to his unjust reward unrepentant and becomes a martyr to his cause—the liberator in death he couldn't be in life whose sacrifice spurs one of the Scottish nobles, Robert the Bruce, to finally win that freedom for their beloved Scotland.

Echoing the finale of *Spartacus*, the doomed Wallace leaves behind a lover pregnant with his child, who will be born in freedom. But the twist here is more ironic, for his lover is the princess of Wales; their child will not only be born free but will be a potential heir to the throne of England as well. Whether this twist is fact or fiction is unimportant. It works sublimely in making us feel that's how things should have been, which is the spirit of all great myths and one that *Braveheart* evokes solidly.

Spartacus can be seen elsewhere in the film, too—in the awesome panoramas of the opposing armies facing each other prior to battle and in the Scottish rebels' ingenious use of fire as a weapon against their better-armed foes. But the battle scenes in *Braveheart* have a

A liberator in death he couldn't be in life. Wallace's sacrifice paves the way for the more cautious and calculating Robert the Bruce to succeed in winning Scotland its freedom.

182

viciousness, especially the scenes of hand-to-hand combat, that *Spartacus* wasn't able to get away with in the 1960s. Most of Kubrick's attempts to re-create the barbarousness of ancient warfare wound up on the cutting-room floor because of censorship restrictions but were later edited back in for the 1991 restoration of the film; the restored footage of limbs being hacked off and other close-range carnage reveals he and Gibson were on the same track.

Such scenes in *Braveheart* are given unflinching treatment; the crash of the English army on horseback into the handmade spears of Wallace's forces is one of the most extraordinary action scenes ever staged for a film. This unflinching treatment is very much to the film's point about Wallace, for whom violence was not just a means to an end but, ultimately, the end itself. Despite his pronouncements that all he wants is to be free and left in peace to farm his land, he lets his vengeful hatred of the British and savage thirst for their blood overtake him, consume him, and become a way of life which finally prevents him from being the one to realize the freedom he desires for Scotland. This is a grave miscalculation Mad Max wouldn't have made, and Robert the Bruce (Angus Macfadyen) doesn't. Gibson reveals this disquieting truth in the rage of the battle scenes and in the breadth of his convincing (impeccable brogue and all), multishaded performance as the doomed hero—a performance somewhat overshadowed by his directorial achievement in *Braveheart* but which is one of the best of his career.

With Sophie Marceau, Wallace's supporter and lover, the princess of Wales. Their child will not only be born free but, in an ironic twist, will become a potential heir to the throne of England as well.

POCAHONTAS

1995—WALT DISNEY PICTURES

"I wouldn't try to make a living at it."
—MEL GIBSON (ON HIS SINGING)

CREDITS

Producer: James Pentecost; *Directors:* Mike Gabriel and Eric Goldberg; *Screenwriters:* Carl Binder, Susannah Grant, and Philip LaZebenik; *Editor:* H. Lee Patterson; *Composer:* Alan Menken; *Lyrics:* Stephen Schwartz; *Art director:* Michael Giaimo.
Running time: 81 minutes.

CAST (VOICES)

Irene Bedard *(Pocahontas);* Judy Kuhn *(Pocahontas [singing voice]);* Mel Gibson *(John Smith);* David Ogden Stiers *(Governor Radcliffe);* John Kassir *(Meeko);* Linda Hunt *(Grandmother Willow);* Russell Means *(Powhatan);* Christian Bale *(Thomas);* David Ogden Stiers *(Wiggins);* Billy Connolly *(Ben);* Joe Baker *(Lon);* Frank Welker *(Flit);* Michelle St. John *(Nakoma);* James Apaumut Fall *(Kocoum);* Gordon Tootoosis *(Kekata).*

REVIEWS

*"*Pocahontas *takes a while to get going, but when it does it becomes a wistful meditation on lost love in what it depicts as the last age of innocence."*
—TIME, 6/19/95

"Even though the studio's traditional strengths are evident, particularly the animation, the story is ultimately unsatisfying, perhaps because even its target audience knows the peace forged by Pocahontas *didn't last happily ever after."*
—MACLEAN'S, 6/26/95

"She [Pocahontas] leaps about the forest, paddles a canoe, and sings of environmental protection. Never before have strip-mining and prejudice been condemned by someone in such a fetching outfit."
—ESQUIRE, 8/95

Capt. John Smith (voiced by Gibson) prefers exploring the new world to plundering it.

ocahontas is a musical-romance with more social commentary but less emotional pull than Disney's *Beauty and the Beast* (1991) and *The Lion King* (1994) and fewer laughs by far than the studio's *Aladdin* (1992). It also has a flimsier story than those animated masterworks. But the stunning graphics are right up there with the best of Disney. In fact, with their breathtaking sense of cinema and extraordinary *mise-en-scène* the studio's animated films in recent years have been putting most of Hollywood's live-action spectaculars to shame, and *Pocohontas* is no exception.

The film is based on the legendary encounter between Pocahontas, daughter of the Indian chief Powhatan, and Capt. John Smith, a soldier-sailor sent to the New World as part of a British expeditionary force to build a settlement called Jamestown (named after the English king) and bring back gold to fill the empire's coffers.

Under the command of Governor Radcliffe, who is out to make a name for himself, the force proceeds to destroy acres of forest and other natural resources in search of the promised gold, striking not pay dirt but fear,

An inveterate "shower singer," Mel Gibson worked extensively with a Disney voice coach to prepare for his offscreen singing debut in Pocahontas.

186

187

then wrath, in the hearts of the Native Americans watching their wilderness home spoiled.

The chance meeting between Pocahontas and Smith, who prefers exploring to plundering, leads to their falling in love—a romance predicted in her dreams. The lovers successfully bridge the cultural gap between them and, like a frontier Romeo and Juliet, try to make their opposing factions come to peaceful terms as well.

This proves difficult when one of Powhatan's braves (and Pocahontas's jealous suitor), Kocoum, is shot and killed by the British during a struggle with Smith. Captured by the Indians, Smith is sentenced to death when all the tribes rally against the invading white men and war threatens to break out.

Feeling duped by Radcliffe's unfulfilled promise of wealth and not wanting to lose their lives for nothing, the villainous governor's forces turn against him and refuse to fight. Seeing his dreams of power and promotion going down the drain if the Indians aren't defeated, Radcliffe grabs a rifle and tries to shoot Powhatan himself, but the chief is saved by Smith, who takes the bullet instead.

Radcliffe is bound in chains by his men and put aboard ship to go back to England. In desperate need of medical attention, Smith must return to England as well. However, the chief assures him he'll always be welcome back in peace. As the film ends, the lovers Pocahontas and Smith tearfully separate, vowing to reunite, though they will never see each other again.

Mel Gibson is in fine speaking *and* singing voice as Capt. John Smith, although, curiously, his character gets to perform no duet with Pocahontas herself. One would have thought a duet between the two lovers obligatory in a romantic film like this, but none is included in the body of the score. There is a male-female duet sung over the closing credits, but the male vocalist isn't Gibson.

Apart from the commercial value of having his name attached to the movie, there's nothing special about the character of Smith to indicate why the Disney folks felt Gibson was such a perfect choice to voice it—unlike, say, the comic-manic genie in *Aladdin*, a character virtually made to order for its vocalist, Robin Williams. Only at the beginning of *Pocahontas* do the filmmakers trade on Gibson's persona in a similar way by having his character, Smith, perform the daring rescue of a shipmate at sea with the kind of reckless disregard for life and limb of a Mad Max or Martin Riggs.

Pocahontas stirred up some controversy upon its release with certain groups, which strongly protested the cartoon's lack of fidelity to the truth behind the Pocahontas–John Smith legend as if it were an Oliver Stone movie.

What this proves, I guess, is that some people have no romance in their bones and lack a sense of proportion and balance as well—which, among others things, is what the movie says, too.

RANSOM

1996—TOUCHSTONE PICTURES

"I love doing the Lethal Weapon *movies, but those can be about the stunts. With this movie, it's about acting."*

—MEL GIBSON

CREDITS

Producers: Scott Rudin, Brian Glazer, and B. Kipling Hagopian; *Director:* Ron Howard; *Screenplay:* Richard Price and Alexander Ignon, based on a screenplay by Cyril Hume and Richard Maibaum; *Cinematographer:* Piotr Sobocinski; *Editors:* Dan Hanley and Michael Hill; *Composer:* James Horner; *Production designer:* Michael Corenblith.
Running time: 121 minutes.

CAST

Mel Gibson *(Tom Mullen);* René Russo *(Kate Mullen);* Brawley Nolte *(Sean Mullen);* Gary Sinise *(Jimmy Shaker);* Lili Taylor *(Maris Connor);* Delroy Lindo *(Agent Lonnie Hawkins);* Live Schreiber *(Clark Barnes);* Donnie Wahlberg *(Cubby Barnes);* Evan Handler *(Miles Roberts);* Nancy Ticotin *(Agent Kimba Welch);* Michael Gaston *(Agent Jack Sickler);* Kevin Neil McCready *(Agent Paul Rhodes);* Paul Guilfoyle *(Wallace);* Allen Bernstein *(Bob Stone);* Dan Hedaya *(Jackie Brown).*

REVIEWS

"Unlike most rugged, square-jawed action-hero stars, Mel Gibson doesn't play it cool. He's the least afraid of showing wild emotion (think of his suicidal ravings in Lethal Weapon, *his rants in* The Bounty), *and in* Ransom *he gets to emote like mad . . ."*

—NEWSWEEK, 11/11/96

*"*Ransom *takes itself very seriously . . . and poor Gibson is called upon at regular intervals to stand and deliver a convincing demonstration of pain. It's a curious sight—all gulps and twitches and clenching of teeth, as if a very small dentist were hard at work inside his head."*

—NEW YORKER, 11/11/96

"[The film's] major sin—a certain ineluctable improbability—is pretty much offset by the moments of winsome humanity [Gibson] finds for his freebooter; by the rich, nicely tuned portrayals of the other actors; and by director Ron Howard's smoothly professional mastery of yet another genre that is new to him."

—TIME, 11/11/96

Mel Gibson and director Ron Howard on the set.

"Gibson has always had a mesmerizing dark side (remember his vengefulness in Mad Max *?), and when his rage catches fire, so does* Ransom.*"*

—*ENTERTAINMENT WEEKLY,* 11/15/96

"It's rare to find a character this disturbingly ambiguous in a mainstream entertainment and Gibson rips into his juicy role with force and feeling."

—*ROLLING STONE,* 11/28/96

Ransom is an exciting and effective thriller with a strong performance by Mel Gibson as the father who strikes back at the kidnappers of his son. But it suffers from a screenplay that tosses in too many ingredients to keep the plot moving and full of surprises, stretching credibility along the way.

The 1956 film of the same name that inspired it was built on a single, intriguing premise. What if the father of a snatched child refused to submit to the kidnappers' demands and used the ransom money to put a bounty on the kidnappers' heads, forcing them into an equally tight squeeze? It is a daring bit of gamesmanship, even though the decision, aimed at getting the child back alive and discouraging other kidnappers, terrifies him.

Everything that happens in the earlier film revolves around this critical decision, about

Tom Mullen has every material element of success. But when his child Sean (Brawley Nolte) is kidnapped, his world is turned upside down. (Young Nolte is actor Nick Nolte's son.)

which there is much anguished discussion before and after it is made. (Except for a brief shot of the arm of one of the kidnappers as he watches TV, we never even see them or learn who they are.) The father is in constant torment as to whether the strategy is the right one or if he's condemned his child to sure death. The authorities oppose the strategy for sound reasons but must help make it work when it becomes a fait accompli. There is much tension between the participants, which is what the story is about, not the kidnappers.

In the remake, Gibson seizes on the decision for reasons that are somewhat obscure and hastily goes right on TV to announce it without

FBI agent Hawkins (Delroy Lindo) instructs Mullen how to handle the kidnapper's call as the phone rings . . . and rings . . . and rings.

sharing his intentions with his wife or the FBI beforehand. Thus, momentum is gained by eliminating a lot of dialogue and creating a helluva surprise, but it also makes the wife irrelevant by forcing her into the role of teary-eyed observer, a curious and dated stance for a film of the 1990s. (In the original, the wife, played by Donna Reed, has been given a potent sedative for nervous exhaustion and is out of commission when the critical life and death decision must be made. When she comes out of it and learns what her husband has done on his own, she turns on him for gambling with their son's life without consulting her and the marriage threatens to collapse, increasing the drama and the tension.)

We know from the start that Tom Mullen (Gibson) a rich airline owner, is a maverick, take-charge kind of guy. Born in upstate New York of humble beginnings, he's built his career on making gutsy decisions, an amusing reference to Gibson's own path to success. But it's a stretch to believe that the character wouldn't at least involve his wife in a critical, life-and-death decision like this one (unlike Reed in the original, she's very much awake and able to be consulted). Doesn't she even merit a say in the matter? She's the child's mother! The change not only undercuts our sympathy for Gibson's character but turns René Russo's role as Kate, Gibson's wife, into a thankless one.

Delroy Lindo's FBI man, Lonnie Hawkins, tells Gibson that the kidnapping is just business to the criminals, not personal, and should be approached that way to ensure the child's safe return. This, too, is an intriguing premise; it presents Gibson's businessman character with the ultimate challenge of his negotiating skills, and for a while the script follows through on it. But then, either worried the audience may become bored or because the filmmakers can't make up their minds, this premise is veered away from and even contradicted.

Without consulting his wife or the FBI agent in charge, the headstrong Mullen uses the ransom money to put a bounty on the kidnappers' heads, believing it the only way to get his son back alive.

192

Taking a cue from Akira Kurosawa's masterful kidnapping drama *High and Low* (1963), the script exposes the kidnapper's motives as psychotically personal, after all. An underpaid cop, embittered by a life of dealing with street scum,

Jimmy Shaker, Gary Sinise's criminal mastermind, resents Gibson's lavish, above-it-all lifestyle and ability to buy his way out of trouble, so he decides to make Gibson pay. It's a twist calculated for momentum only; as soon as it comes,

The kidnappers put the anguished Mullen through a rigorous workout during the ransom drop, forcing him to rush from one place to another in record time.

ing on the needs of the moment. Models of supercool professionalism and efficiency in one scene, the feds become incompetent stumblebums in the next. Gibson has been instructed by the kidnapper not to call in the FBI. He goes against these instructions, but to keep their arrival a secret, the feds show up at the building disguised as cleaning people. Once inside Gibson's penthouse apartment, however, they parade before the windows seemingly unconcerned about, or not having considered, the possibility that the kidnappers may be watching from one of the dozens of nearby high-rises that command a full view of the place.

Later, Lindo waits until the first ransom call is made to give Gibson lengthy instructions as to how to handle it. Suspense builds nicely as Lindo babbles on and the phone rings and rings, but surely the kidnappers would be alerted that something was amiss when the anxious parents didn't snatch up the phone on the first ring—and the FBI man would want to avoid this.

Perhaps because Gibson had a great deal of input into the script, his Tom Mullen is the one character in the film who doesn't undergo a lot of similarly contradictory transformations calculated for dramatic effect. He remains fairly consistent. And Gibson makes the most of his role. The scene in which he breaks down with guilt, shame, and even contemplates suicide when he believes he's killed his own son by pushing the kidnapper too far is a real tour de force.

Sinise's crafty kidnapper turns so pathologically inept that the sophisticated scheme he has so far planned and executed with care suddenly crumbles like a house of cards.

The FBI gets the same treatment, depend-

The film had the opportunity to be the same. But by constantly going for the gusto rather than the heart or the mind, *Ransom* instead winds up being just an entertaining and often gripping couple of hours.

CONSPIRACY THEORY

WARNER BROS./1997

"I found the subject matter intriguing. As far as conspiracy theories go, I give some credence to them. I have no doubt that there's a covert force at work somewhere, keeping things undercover and admitting only certain things to the public."

—MEL GIBSON

CREDITS

Producers: Joel Silver and Richard Donner; *Director:* Richard Donner; *Screenplay:* Brian Helgeland; *Cinematographer:* John Schwartzman; *Editors:* Frank J. Urioste and Kevin Stitt; *Composer:* Carter Burwell; *Production designer:* Paul Sylbert;
Running time: 135 minutes.

CAST

Mel Gibson *(Jerry Fletcher)*; Julia Roberts *(Alice Sutton)*; Patrick Stewart *(Dr. Jonas)*; Cylk Cozart *(Agent Lowry)*; Stephen Kahan *(Wilson)*; Terry Alexander *(Flip)*; Alex McArthur *(Cynic)*; Donal Gibson *(Doctor—Roosevelt Hospital)*.

Reviews

"Although the actor is playing yet another unhinged character, Gibson outdoes himself. . . [he] has a truly daunting task and triumphs in one of his best roles. The actor's technique has evolved to a high level."

—HOLLYWOOD REPORTER, 8/4/97

"Gibson is very good as the film opens, delivering a classic, motormouth monologue of conspiracy theories that is a hoot."

—CHICAGO TRIBUNE, 8/8/97

"Gibson, delivering one of the hearty, dynamic star turns that have made him the Peter Pan of the blockbuster set, makes Jerry much more boyishly likable than he deserves to be."

—THE NEW YORK TIMES, 8/8/97

*Julia Roberts and Mel Gibson—*Conspiracy Theory's *two "birds on a wire."*

Left to right: *Director Richard Donner, producer Joel Silver, Patrick Stewart, Mel Gibson, and Julia Roberts on the set of* Conspiracy Theory.

On the set of Assassins, the 1995 Sylvestor Stallone action-thriller he'd written for producer Joel Silver, screenwriter Brian Helgeland was asked by Silver if he had any other high concept ideas for a follow-up. Helgeland said he had a story percolating about a paranoid guy who imagines conspiracies at every level of society and expounds upon his theories in a newsletter he distributes to a small list of like-minded wackos gotten off the Internet. The protagonist is like the boy who cried wolf; no one believes him until he accidentally hits upon a real conspiracy and the bad guys show up to silence him. Feeling the story required some "heart" in order to sustain audience interest in a character who is so seriously disturbed that his behavior is somewhat off-putting, Helgeland decided to combine that story with another one he was working on about a guy who is hopelessly in love with a woman he cannot have.

Silver commissioned Helgeland to write the script, which they took to action director Richard Donner. All three agreed that Mel Gibson was the only actor with the range and appeal needed to make this loser of a character seem like a winner and, therefore, draw a big audience.

Gibson read the script and saw in Jerry Fletcher, the paranoid taxi-driver protagonist, a character who possessed all the qualities intrinsic to his acting interests. The role was the lead but it was a character part first and foremost. Furthermore, the character was so mentally damaged by his paranoia, his emotional development so arrested, that his behavior was often alienating. This provided Gibson with the kind of acting challenge he likes. So, he quickly signed on. It was he who pushed for Julia Roberts to costar as the reluctant object of Fletcher's love, a Justice Department lawyer who gets involved in uncovering the conspiracy with him. With Roberts on board, Warner Bros. jumped at financing the film, viewing the combination of Mel Gibson (playing yet another over-the-edge loose cannon), Donner, Roberts, comedy, action and thrills as a potential blockbuster—an unofficial *Lethal Weapon 4.*

The completed film, appropriately titled *Conspiracy Theory,* was scheduled for release on

Mel Gibson prepares for a scene where his character is strapped into a hospital bed and will soon die at the hands of the conspirators if Alice doesn't come to his rescue.

Alice (Julia Roberts) and Jerry (Mel Gibson) escape their pursuers by hopping a bus, where they discuss the mysterious deaths of his conspiracy newsletter subscribers.

July 25, 1997, the same date as another potential Warner Bros. blockbuster, the action-thriller *Air Force One* starring Harrison Ford. Ford, whose box office appeal and clout with the studios is up there with Gibson's, questioned the wisdom of having the studio's two major summer releases go head-to-head on the same date. He urged Warner Bros. execs to push back the release of Conspiracy Theory and release *Air Force One*, which had been completed first, on July 25. Some insiders suggest that Ford threatened not to make any more films for the

studio if his request was not agreed to. Whatever the reason, the studio relented and the release of *Conspiracy Theory* was delayed until August 8.

Perhaps the studio execs simply flipped a coin. Or maybe they just looked at the two films and decided the exciting but by-the-numbers *Air Force One* was a more surefire hit whereas *Conspiracy Theory*, the participation of Gibson, Roberts, and Donner notwithstanding, was more iffy—which, as it turns out, is the case, for *Conspiracy Theory* is a very mixed bag indeed.

Mel Gibson's Jerry Fletcher is a man whose obsession with conspiracies stems from the fear of a past he can't remember. That past is tied to Roberts's Alice Sutton — for whom Jerry is a self-appointed guardian angel with romantic intentions. Curiously, in one of the film's many lapses of logic, Alice, whose father was murdered under circumstances the official explanation of which she is unable to accept, is never in any real jeopardy until guardian angel Jerry gets her neck-deep in trouble as the result of his paranoia. Even then, the threat is never terribly menacing or suspenseful due to the ease with which the two elude the none-too-bright and woefully ostentatious (for shadowy conspirators) bad guys hot on their trail.

The conspiracy Jerry uncovers, and of which he is revealed to be a part as his past comes back to haunt him, involves a government psychiatrist (Patrick Stewart in a lackluster performance due to his one-dimensional, underwritten role) with former ties to CIA brainwashing experiments. For years, Dr. Jonas has been programming ordinary guys to be assassins for high-paying freelance hits. Jerry's was a failed experiment and he must be terminated for his knowledge, however buried in his subconscious that knowledge may be. There's nothing new here, of course; it's straight out of *The Manchurian Candidate* (1962), which the film openly acknowledges. However, the film is given an intriguing twist by the use of J.D. Salinger's classic novel *Catcher in the Rye* as a combination trigger device (similar to *Candidate*'s playing cards) and phony explanation for the assassins' motives and mindset. In the event they are caught, authorities can explain that the assasins are just wacko lone gunmen driven by an unhealthy identification with Salinger's angst-ridden protagonist, Holden Caulfield, like real-life assassins Mark David Chapman (John Lennon's killer) and John W. Hinckley (the shooter of President Reagan) in whose possession copies of Salinger's novel were actually found. But with the exception of this twist, *Conspiracy*'s conspiracy is fairly routine stuff. It works okay because formula usually does.

What doesn't work very well is the love

Director Richard Donner discusses an upcoming scene with Mel Gibson and Julia Roberts on the set of Conspiracy Theory.

Alice (Julia Roberts) orders the police to back off from kicking Jerry (Mel Gibson) around after the paranoid but seemingly harmless man pushes his way into the Justice Department wielding a gun.

despite Gibson's inherent likability as a performer. Gibson strives mightily to make us care about Jerry too, but in the end succeeds mainly in making us put up with him. In a performance that occasionally threatens to slip over the edge into manic self-parody, Gibson stretches the audience's support of his bonkers character a bit too far and that support finally gives way. While we never turn against Jerry, we never really become involved with him, or his plight, either. The character is such a basket case, his paranoia (however justified it proves to be) so galloping, his nervous twitches, mutterings, and running off at the mouth about conspiracies (and everything else) so incessant, that he becomes, well, *exhausting*. At one point, Roberts's Alice gives voice to her, as well as our own, exhaustion with Jerry when she impatiently begs him, "Jerry, *slow down!*" The subsequent breather is fleeting, but most welcome nonetheless.

Warner Bros. may have been hoping for a *Lethal Weapon 4*, but what it got was a way too overlong variation of *Bird on a Wire* in which Jack Schwartzman's Oscar-worthy cinematography is the standout feature. The opening scene, a parody of Martin Scorsese's *Taxi Driver* (1976), where Jerry prattles on about the nature of conspiracies to his customers (one of them Richard Donner, doing a cameo similar to Scorsese's in the earlier film) as his cab prowls the rain-slicked, neon-glittering streets of New York is breathtaking.

story between Jerry and Alice that Helgeland brought in to give the movie "heart." It comes across as a second thought because there is no emotional resonance to it, except at the tearful conclusion, which the filmmakers immediately negate in an epilogue for which there is little rationale except that it serves to end the movie on a happier note.

What "heart" there is in *Conspiracy Theory* is generated mostly by Julia Roberts who touchingly manages to make her character's concern for the disarmingly lunatic Jerry convincing, even though we don't quite come to share it

As this book goes to press, Mel Gibson has

Mel Gibson as Jerry Fletcher, a man obsessed with conspiracies and haunted by the fear of a past he cannot remember.

announced that his next film will be *Point Blank*, a remake of the 1967 film of the same name about a revenge-seeking killer, based on the novel *The Hunter* by Richard Stark (Donald E. Westlake). The film will mark the directorial debut of its writer, Brian Helgeland, who promises not to add any "heart" this time. In fact, Mel Gibson, who remains committed to stretching the audience's support in his choice of roles, says he signed to do the picture because his character (played by Lee Marvin in the earlier version) is "so completely venal and heartless."

Now *that's* going against type!

LETHAL WEAPON 4

1998—WARNER BROS.

"It is a bit like episodic TV, isn't it?"
—MEL GIBSON

CREDITS

Producers: Joel Silver, Richard Donner; *Director:* Richard Donner; *Screenwriter:* Channing Gibson, from a story by Jonathan Lemkin, Alfred Gough, Miles Millar, based on characters created by Shane Black; *Cinematographer:* Andrzej Bartkowiak; *Editors:* Dallas Puett, Kevin Stitt, Eric Strand, Frank J. Urioste; *Composers:* Michael Kamen, Eric Clapton, Marcus Miller, David Sanborn; *Production designer:* J. Michael Riva; Running time: 127 minutes.

CAST

Mel Gibson *(Martin Riggs);* Danny Glover *(Roger Murtaugh);* Joe Pesci *(Leo Getz);* Rene Russo *(Lorna Cole);* Chris Rock *(Lee Butters);* Jet Li *(Wah Sing Ku);* Steve Kahan *(Captain Ed Murphy);* Kim Chan *(Uncle Benny);* Darlene Love *(Trish Murtaugh);* Traci Wolfe *(Rianne);* Eddy Ko *(Hong);* Steven Lam *(Ping);* Richard Libertini *(Rabbi).*

REVIEWS

"If we get the movies we deserve, what have we done to be worthy of Lethal Weapon 4*? A fourth-generation copy of a distant original,* Lethal 4 *is less a movie than a habit. Like a too-long-running TV show, it makes a fetish of familiarity, featuring the usual faces doing one more time what they've done repeatedly in the past."*

—LOS ANGELES TIMES, 7/10/98

"Detectives Riggs and Murtaugh are up to the sort of mischief in Lethal Weapon 4 *that's made the series a successful popcorn entertainment over the past decade. The quintessence of the buddy cop pic,* LW4 *is big on action, playful banter, and just enough plot to keep our attention from wandering. It matters little that the film is rife with non sequiturs, nonsense, and nihilistic violence, because its heroes are so darn buoyant and charming."*

—VARIETY, 7/8/98

"In Lethal Weapon 4, *about the only thing that's changed between stable family man Roger Murtaugh*

After years of saying "Never again!" Mel Gibson reprises the role of loose cannon L.A. cop Martin Riggs in another case, this one involving gangsters, a counterfeiting racket, corrupt Chinese military officials, a Hong Kong Triad, and much, much more.

and hot-wired widower Martin Riggs since Lethal Weapon 3 *is that the bantering, bickering LAPD partners have gotten older, just as the actors themselves have thickened in middle age. Why not give the guys a nice party and let them retire these roles with dignity?"*

—ENTERTAINMENT WEEKLY, 7/10/98

"With this latest episode in the adventures of nutty cop Martin Riggs and uptight cop Roger Murtaugh, the series has become as schizoid as Riggs, jumping all over the place and encompassing every genre.

One moment, it's a frat boy comedy, with Gibson playing tricks on Glover; the next moment, it's a high-tech action movie with planes, trains, and automobiles mangling bodies. Then it's a sentimental drama about family values. Then it's an action film again. Chris Rock and Joe Pesci drop by for a few stand-up routines, there's more action, and then the film quiets down so that Gibson and Glover can do some soul searching about aging. Call them Grumpy Old Cops. In short, it's a mess, albeit a weirdly entertaining mess."

—SACRAMENTO BEE, 7/10/98

Pinned down by a lunatic with a more firepower than an NRA convention, Riggs (Mel Gibson) crazily suggests to his long-suffering partner that Murtaugh (Danny Glover) strip and flap arms like a chicken to distract the lunatic long enough for Riggs to get the drop on him.

At one point, after defying his umpteenth brush with Looney Tunes–style death, Mel Gibson's Martin Riggs turns to his longtime, long-suffering, *still-not-retired* partner Roger Murtaugh (Danny Glover) and utters Murtaugh's signature line from the other films in the series:

"I'm too old for this shit," Riggs confesses.

We understand what he means because what was true of *Lethal Weapon 3* is even truer of *Lethal Weapon 4.* It's one *Lethal Weapon* movie too many—*way too many.*

Everything about this latest installment in the series is excessive—from the ongoing banter between the two cop buddies, which is ratch-

eted up here to nonstop (and is often indecipherable over the noisy pyrotechnics), to the video game violence, which is wall-to-wall, to the Byzantine plot. While money may have talked in getting the stars to commit to another go-round as Riggs and Murtaugh (after years of saying, "Never again!"), the film's plot may have been another incentive. There's certainly no lack of it. *Lethal Weapon 4* has more plot than the first three movies combined. There are so many different threads going off in so any different directions that it becomes a near impossibility keeping track of them all. Here's just a sampling:

• Riggs is living with Lorna (Rene Russo),

Riggs attempts to board a truck the hard way in a wild freeway pursuit—the film's hair-raising high point.

who is pregnant and wants their child born in wedlock. But Riggs is fearful of marriage because he hasn't come to terms yet with the loss of his first wife, who died, he admits painfully, because of his being a cop.

● Murtaugh's grown daughter Rianne is also pregnant, but she won't reveal the name of the father (Chris Rock) whom she has secretly married because Murtaugh will disapprove of his being a cop.

● Internal Affairs suspects Murtaugh of being on the take because he's throwing around more money lately than his cop salary provides.

● Chinese gangsters are smuggling cheap labor into the city on Riggs and Murtaugh's watch.

● These same gangsters are involved in a counterfeiting racket aimed at paying off some corrupt Chinese military officials who are holding four top members of a Hong Kong Triad for ransom here in the States.

No wonder it took a team of writers to get all this down on paper!

The *Lethal Weapon* films have endured as a successful franchise not because of their complex plots and multidimensional characters, however, but because of their winning formula, which combines high-octane thrills with laughs. The formula may be running on fumes in *Lethal Weapon 4*, but it's still chugging.

Similar to increasing the banter between Riggs and Murtaugh to nonstop, the filmmakers step up the mayhem to near nonstop as well. A tanker truck, two cars, a yacht, and a freighter are ear-splittingly demolished in whole or in part (and one loses count of how many people are killed in the process) before the film is barely seventeen minutes old. Despite the zip these sequences have, there is, however, a been-there-seen-that (in the first three films and a zillion other action movies) feel to them that is wearing, as well as wearying.

But occasionally the filmmakers manage to surprise us by pulling an action scene out of the hat that actually takes our breath away.

For example, there's a wild freeway chase in *Lethal Weapon 4* that is truly hair-raising (as well as quite funny). And in the film's most vio-lent action sequence, the vicious martial arts duel at the conclusion with villain Jet Li, Mel Gibson's Riggs takes his worst pounding since the climax of *Lethal Weapon 2* before he finally emerges gruesomely victorious.

Laughs (as opposed to silliness) are not as plentiful this time around, but *Lethal Weapon 4* does have its share of them—thanks mostly to Joe Pesci, reprising his motor-mouthed Leo Getz character (who has now turned private eye), and stand-up comedian Chris Rock in his acting debut. They're funny enough separately, but a stitch as a duo in the film's funniest scene where the two of them go off on a rant about cell phones.

Lethal Weapon 4 probably hasn't won Mel Gibson any new fans, though it likely hasn't cost him any old ones, either. But it's time to push on rather than keep pushing the luck—or, as Roger Murtaugh might say, "Enough already, Riggs!"

PAYBACK

1999—PARAMOUNT PICTURES

"Any character you portray, you have to understand at some level, and therefore it is an aspect of you. It may be a really dark recessive corner of who you are, or a simple imagining that you can make real for yourself, but it's you."

—MEL GIBSON

CREDITS

Producer: Bruce Davey; *Director:* Brian Helgeland;
Screenwriters: Brian Helgeland and Terry Hayes, based
on the novel *The Hunter* by Donald E. Westlake writing
as "Richard Stark"; *Cinematographer:* Ericson Core;
Editor: Kevin Stitt; *Composer:* Chris Boardman;
Production designer: Richard Hoover;
Running time: 102 minutes.

CAST

Mel Gibson *(Porter);* Gregg Henry *(Val Resnick);* Maria
Bello *(Rosie);* David Paymer *(Arthur Stegman);* Bill Duke
(Detective Hicks); Deborah Kara Unger *(Mrs. Lynn Porter);*
John Glover *(Phil);* William Devane *(Carter);* Lucy Alexis
Liu *(Pearl);* Jack Conley *(Detective Leary);* Kris Kristofferson
(Bronson); James Coburn *(Justin Fairfax, uncredited).*

REVIEWS

*"Gibson, unlike, say, Clint Eastwood, has such
instinctive wry enthusiasm as an actor that when
he attempts to hold back every last drop of human
feeling, it doesn't render him particularly scary or
charismatic. Mostly, he seems depressed, like a guy
who has turned to violence out of pure morose
indifference."*

—ENTERTAINMENT WEEKLY, 2/5/99

*"Venal though he may be, Porter is that old friend,
a thief with a sense of honor, and Gibson plays the
combination of sad-sack Everyman and avenging
angel to the hilt. Breathing tobacco smoke like
oxygen, he narrates the tale with a rumbling Ray-
mond Chandleresque voice-over that has him dropping such hard-boiled bons mots as 'Old habits die
hard. If you don't kick them they kick you.'"*

—WASHINGTON POST, 2/5/99

*"Gibson carries such an established screen image—
and a bag of mannerisms—that it's almost impossible to watch his performance without thinking of the
Lethal Weapon movies. Holding the episodic, occasionally disjointed picture on his shoulders, he renders a decent performance, nothing more."*

—VARIETY, 2/5/99

*"Payback is a bloody good remake of John Boor-
man's 1967 thriller* Point Blank, *which featured a
snarling Lee Marvin. As an antihero, Mr. Gibson
lacks Mr. Marvin's bullying frame, but he flourishes
with a wry, cutting wit. The sometimes hammy box-
office star has rarely seemed less intent on wooing*

Porter (Mel Gibson) and his partner Val (Gregg Henry) clock the transfer of the Chinese mob money they plan to rip off.

the audience. His performance indicates that he might remain a strong presence even after growing too old to be 'cute.' "

—DALLAS MORNING NEWS, 2/5/99

Having stretched audience sympathy for his character in *Conspiracy Theory* to the breaking point (some said past it), Mel Gibson decided the time was right to play a villain—in the British sense of the word, i.e., the bad guy but not *the* bad guy. He'd played numerous characters with dark sides throughout his career and not suffered any loss of audience. Why not tackle one who *embraced* the dark side, and see if he could still make the audience go with him?

The vehicle Mel chose for this tightrope walk was a 1963 novel by Richard Stark (Donald E. Westlake) called *The Hunter.* The book was one of a series Stark wrote about a career crook named Parker. In this one, Parker is double-crossed and left for dead by his partner after a successful heist. But Parker recovers from his wounds and sets out to get back his share of the money.

The Hunter was previously filmed in 1967 as *Point Blank,* starring Lee Marvin as Parker, whose name was changed for some reason to Walker (and would be changed yet again for some other reason to Porter in the Gibson remake). *Point Blank* is considered by many film buffs and critics to be a seminal thriller of the late 1960s because of the elliptical, nonlinear style of its narrative, an antihero protagonist who's as violent as the guys and gals who wrong him, and a nihilistic ending where nobody wins. These qualities made it one of the strongest and most influential forebears of the ultraviolent, (mostly) urban crime thriller genre in the mold of the classic films noir of the 1940s that has come to be known as "neo-noir." The string of such films continues unbroken to this day with

In only a few scenes do we get a glimpse of the frightening heart of darkness in the character Gibson set out to portray.

movies like *Conspiracy Theory, L.A. Confidential,* and now *Payback,* a loose update of the film that helped to start the ball rolling.

Interestingly, all three of these later "neo-noirs" were scripted or co-scripted by Brian Helgeland, who made his directorial debut with *Payback.* In fact, *Payback* began as his baby. He'd been working on the script during the making of *Conspiracy Theory.* Gibson asked him what he was up to, the writer showed him, Mel saw they were on the same wavelength, and he signed on to play Porter with Helgeland at the helm. Gibson's own company, Icon Productions, would produce the film for Paramount Pictures.

Their meeting of the minds failed to survive the making of the movie, however. An early cut of *Payback* set off an alarm bell to Gibson and the Icon and Paramount brass that the badass Porter was *so* badass it was hard to root for him. If general audiences reacted similarly, the film's planned advertising campaign ("Get ready to root for the bad guy") would tank, and so might the film.

Suggesting that Helgeland's script followed the same nihilistic path of Stark's book and *Point Blank,* the finale of this early cut of the film was judged by Gibson and company to be stillborn and confusing. They decided some major rewrites were necessary.

Helgeland was offered the opportunity to do the rewrites and direct the new scenes, but he declined, claiming the changes would compromise his artistic vision, and he departed the project. At which point Terry Hayes, a writer pal of Gibson's from the old *Mad Max* days who was doing a rewrite of Ray Bradbury's script for Gibson's *Fahrenheit 451* remake, was asked to step in and develop the new material for *Payback.*

Ultimately, Helgeland and Hayes would share screenplay credit, and Helgeland would receive sole director credit, though approximately a third of the film was reshot after he left by another director (an uncredited Mel Gibson, it has been rumored).

An already-shot scene where Porter gives his addict wife (Deborah Kara Unger) a vicious beating for double-crossing him with his partner was cut from the film in the belief (probably correct) that it would turn most women in the audience against Gibson's character completely. A prologue was added portraying the heist and the double-cross to help "justify" Porter's subsequent actions. And the last third of the movie was rewritten and reshot to include a scene clearly designed to arouse audience sympathy for Porter where he's worked over with a hammer by the badder guys, and a *Mission Impossible*–style finale where Porter cleverly engineers the destruction of every gangster and corrupt cop he's up against, and gets away

Porter catches up with Val (Gregg Henry), relaxing after some strenuous S&M with dominatrix-for-hire Pearl (Lucy Liu), and demands his share of the money back.

Porter (Mel Gibson) steps out of "neo-noir" into the world of the Hong Kong action film to get even with all comers, John Woo–style.

not only with his share of the money but the entire score.

Though perhaps more crowd-pleasing, *Payback*'s revised ending undermines Porter's motives and the code that drives them. As his quest is to get back only what's his, this sudden winner-take-all turnabout makes his character a muddle. What kind of payback does he really want: his rightful share of the ill-gotten loot as he keeps saying, or brutal revenge against any and all comers? Is he the Terminator? Or is he a thug with a skewed sense of righteous indignation about what is his, what isn't, and the hell he'll go through to claim it that confounds his greedy adversaries because they can't believe anyone could be "that dumb?" We can believe the latter of Lee Marvin's single-minded but not overly bright Walker in *Point Blank* because of the look of incomprehension that consistently crosses his face whenever someone suggests a different motive for his actions. *Payback* estab-

lishes the same scenario (though it's difficult to accept Mel Gibson's Porter as being even remotely "dumb"). But then it shifts gears by turning the character, especially in the last third of the film, into a killing machine—a deadpan avenger, cleverer by half than anyone else, but just as greedy—whom the filmmakers program to give the audience an orgy of Hong Kong–style action-movie kicks.

Only in isolated (presumably untouched) scenes—like the one where Porter wastes his deceitful partner with a sudden and chilling dispassion after getting the information he wants about the money's location—do we get a glimpse of the frightening heart of darkness in the character that Gibson and Helgeland set out in the beginning to explore. If there had been more of this in *Payback* the movie might have been a genuine "neo-noir" rather than the sendup of one that it ultimately turns out to be.

CHICKEN RUN

2000—DREAMWORKS PICTURES

"You can't be afraid to look like an idiot when you act this stuff out in front of a microphone. Which is no problem. I've looked like an idiot for many years now."

—MEL GIBSON

CREDITS

Producers: Peter Lord, David Sproxton, Nick Park; *Directors:* Peter Lord, Nick Park; *Screenwriter:* Karey Kirkpatrick, based on a story by Nick Park, Peter Lord; *Cinematographers;* Dave Alex Riddett, Tristan Oliver, Frank Passingham; *Editor:* Mark Solomon; *Composers:* John Powell, Harry Gregson-Williams, Steve Jablonsky, James McKee Smith, Geoff Zanelli; *Production designer:* Phil Lewis; Running time: 85 minutes.

CAST

Mel Gibson *(Rocky Roads);* Julia Sawalha *(Ginger);* Miranda Richardson *(Mrs. Tweedy);* Jane Horrocks *(Babs);* Lynn Ferguson *(Mac);* Imelda Staunton *(Bunty);* Benjamin Whitrow *(Fowler);* Tony Haygarth *(Mr. Tweedy);* Phil Daniels *(Fletcher the Rat);* Timothy Spall *(Nick the Rat);* John Sharian *(Circus Man).*

REVIEWS

"Mel Gibson brings his expected energy and an antic, boisterous humor to the cocky Rocky."

—VARIETY, 6/12/00

"Dropping in, literally, on this self-described 'group of rather desperate chickens' is [an] American rooster [named] Rocky (wonderfully done by Mel Gibson), a confident Rhode Island Red who's done 'that whole barnyard thing' and now considers himself something of a 'Lone Free Ranger.' "

—LOS ANGELES TIMES, 6/21/00

"Each chicken is a miracle of characterization, and the tour-de-force sequence—in which the heroine and the Yank hero (Mel Gibson, never funnier) fight to stay in one piece in a pie-making machine with more wheels, cogs, and pulleys than Rube Goldberg's worst nightmare—surpasses Indiana Jones and the Temple of Doom *(1984) for sheer kinetic marvelousness."*

—SLATE, 6/23/00

"Mel Gibson's voice supplies Rocky with all the wiseguy lingo he needs until the jig is up and he has to rebuild his credibility fast after an old RAF rooster named Fowler invokes the World War II British resentment against pushy Yanks who were rather more forward with the local women than the lads deemed sporting."

—BOSTON GLOBE, 6/23/00

Rocky "the lone free ranger" Roads (voiced by Mel Gibson) gets a harsh reminder of why he's needed by the desperate chickens of Tweedy's Farm.

No computer-generated images (CGI) for these guys! It's the hands-on approach for cinemagicians Nick Park, Peter Lord, and their cohorts at Britain's Aardman Studios. These folks continue to animate the old-fashioned way, the same way it was done when the movies were born: filming one drawing at a time, or, in Aardman's case, one small movement of a 3-D clay figure at a time (stop-motion claymation, the process is called).

Why should they go "higher-tech?" Their work has already scored three Academy Awards in the Best Animated Short Film category (for 1989's *A Grand Day Out,* 1993's *The Wrong Trousers,* and 1995's *A Close Shave*) plus Aardman has produced an animated TV show that's become a worldwide cult hit. The latter is named *Wallace and Gromit* after its clay superstars—a wacky, absentminded inventor and his whip-smart, put-upon pooch, respectively; Wallace and Gromit also top-billed Aardman's Oscar-winning shorts.

There's no arguing with success. For its maiden voyage into the uncharted waters of feature film animation, Aardman scored several more coups by adhering to their old ways. Park,

Mr. And Mrs. Tweedy (voiced by Tony Haygarth and Miranda Richardson) do a beak count to make sure none of the inmates have escaped from Tweedy's Egg Farm.

Lord, and Company got Steven Spielberg's DreamWorks studios to put up the money, and landed Mel Gibson to voice the male lead. Aardman and Gibson were not previously acquainted. Aardman just sent Gibson the script on a hunch, and that hunch proved solid. Gibson loved the concept of a World War II POW escape movie set on a British chicken farm—with all the clichés of the genre intact (and turned on their ear)—to be a hoot, and said yes to voicing the part of Rocky Roads, his first starring role in an animated feature since Disney's *Pocahontas*; and this time he wouldn't have to sing (albeit briefly)!

As it turns out, Mel Gibson brings more than his voice to *Chicken Run*. In many ways the part he plays—a cocky Yank rooster—is not only a feathered send-up of the type of cocky Yank characters played by the likes of Steve McQueen and Sylvester Stallone in such films as *The Great Escape* and *Victory*, but a self-deprecating turn

on his own iconic screen image (and a warmup for his role in *What Women Want* to boot).

The plucky POWs of Tweedy's Farm are in desperate straits. It's the chopping block if egg production falls too low—and now there's an even more menacing threat on the horizon: a monstrous chicken-pie-making machine. Spurred on by the determined Ginger, the chicks make one escape attempt after another, but to no avail. What they need to achieve freedom, Ginger realizes, is a miracle—at which point that miracle drops from the sky in the form of Rocky Roads, a flying rooster full of braggadocio about an unfettered life.

"Where are you from?" one of the dimmer chickens asks the Yank intruder.

"The land of the free, the home of the brave," he answers.

"Ah, Scotland!" a proud fowl pipes up in a tongue-in-cheek nod to Mel Gibson's epic paean to freedom, *Braveheart.*

216

Pampered by the hens at Tweedy's Farm, Rocky (voiced by Mel Gibson), in tub, has it made as long as he can keep up his macho hero charade.

Having hurt his wing in the fall, Rocky needs a place to hide out (he's an escapee from a circus) until he's fully healed and can take to the open road again. Tweedy's Farm seems a good bet because he can be the pampered object of affection to "all these beautiful English chicks" while recuperating. But Ginger strikes a hard bargain. Unless he agrees to help them make a break for it by teaching them to fly like he can, she'll blow the whistle on him.

Rocky strings Ginger and the other chickens along with unsuccessful flying lessons until the time comes when he must either put up or shut up. By now his wing is healed though, and he pulls a fade, leaving behind part of an old circus poster of his for Ginger to find, which reveals that he's a fraud: He can't fly, except when fired from a circus cannon.

With the pie-making machine finally up and running, the countdown is on for Ginger to dig deep into her resourcefulness and come up with a foolproof escape plan.

Thanks to a memento that Rocky also left behind for her, she seizes on an idea that finally takes the feathered POWs (plus a couple of helpful rats) over the fence to freedom. It's no wonder Mel Gibson responded well to the script of *Chicken Run*; it echoes a familiar refrain from many of his other films, particularly *Braveheart*. Here again, it is the character played by Gibson who inspires achievement in others.

217

THE PATRIOT

2000—COLUMBIA PICTURES

"I've seen the epics, and some of them don't touch you on an emotional or human level at all. While this is a very big film, the far more important story is the one of the people, the family, which is something everyone can relate to. If that works, you can have as many cannon blasts as you like because then they mean something."

—MEL GIBSON

CREDITS

Producers: Dean Devlin, Mark Gordon, Gary Levinsohn; *Director:* Roland Emmerich; *Screenwriter:* Robert Rodat; *Cinematographer:* Caleb Deschanel; *Editor:* David Brenner; *Composer:* John Williams; *Production designer:* Kirk M. Petruccelli; Running time: 164 minutes.

CAST

Mel Gibson *(Benjamin Martin);* Heath Ledger *(Gabriel Martin);* Joely Richardson *(Charlotte Selton);* Jason Isaacs *(Colonel William Tavington);* Chris Cooper *(Colonel Harry Burwell);* Tcheky Karyo *(Jean Villeneuve);* Rene Auberjonois *(Reverend Oliver);* Tom Wilkinson *(Lord Cornwallis);* Lisa Brenner *(Anne Patricia Howard);* Adam Baldwin *(Captain Wilkins);* Donal Logue *(Dan Scott);* Mika Boorem *(Margaret Martin);* Logan Lerman *(William Martin);* Trevor Morgan *(Nathan Martin);* Skye McCole Bartusiak *(Susan Martin);* Mary Jo Deschanel *(Mrs. Howard).*

REVIEWS

"Built on a shaky foundation of generic characters, stilted dialogue, shallow platitudes about war and peace and a steadfast belief that any scene not featuring star Mel Gibson is a waste of celluloid, The Patriot *is a thoroughly unconvincing rewrite of American history whose singular lack of subtlety may prompt unintended laughs. Gibson gives a mechanically precise but soulless performance in which he seems more concerned with how he looks than what his character is thinking or feeling."*

—HOLLYWOOD REPORTER, 6/16/00

"Corny and melodramatic as it is, The Patriot *still manages to do something few films have done—to tell a story of the American Revolutionary War that has some emotional pull and isn't stuffy and dull. Gibson (a man with seven kids himself, we can't forget) forcefully socks over the two prime components of his role, the deeply caring dad who would just like to watch his children grow up in peace, and the vengeful, crafty warrior capable of great brutality."*

—VARIETY, 6/16/00

"Some people won't be able to dig out the poignant reality beneath what looks superficially like rather old-fashioned spectacle. But that, perhaps, is why Mel Gibson was placed on earth. He is hard pressed here—by family losses, by the unrelieved harshness

Mel Gibson as retired warrior turned pater familias Benjamin Martin in The Patriot.

Benjamin (Mel Gibson) is unable to prevent the off-screen death of his second oldest son, Thomas, who is cold-bloodedly executed for trying to intervene in Gabriel's arrest.

of this nasty, backwoods war, by the demons that haunt his character. Yet we are never unaware of the actor's fundamental good nature, reflected in Martin's fierce, sweet love of family, the casual ease of his action passages."

—*Time*, 6/26/00

"Gibson plays Martin as a man conscience-stricken by his own savagery when he fought in the French and Indian War, afraid of reaping a harvest of bad karma. There's something dark and reined-in about Gibson's Martin. He's afraid of his own capacity for violence. When he does go to war, and his

weapon of choice turns out to be the tomahawk, we're not surprised by his proficiency with it—or by the frequency with which he's drenched in his enemies' blood."

—*Boston Globe*, 6/28/00

Mel Gibson's intention was to return to the director's chair with his next project, the long-in-gestation remake of *Fahrenheit 451*. But continued rewrite problems put the sci-fi epic again on hold, maybe permanently—at least with Mel Gibson at the helm;

Once on opposite sides of the war debate, Gabriel (Heath Ledger) and his father Benjamin (Mel Gibson) now share a common goal—the defeat of the British and revenge against the brutal Colonel Tavington; but not necessarily in that order, according to Benjamin.

rumors have since abounded that producer-director Frank Darabont will be taking over the project.

Instead, Gibson returned to the screen as the star of *The Patriot,* a sprawling epic of the American Revolution in the stirringly patriotic mode of *Independence Day,* the stirringly patriotic sci-fi epic of a few summers earlier from the same producer-director team of Dean Devlin and Roland Emmerich.

Gibson plays widower Benjamin Martin, a veteran of the French and Indian Wars who now leads a quiet life as a South Carolina gentleman farmer and father to his seven motherless children. But his violent past comes back to haunt him when the American fight for independence from England literally reaches his doorstep—a brutal battle between the ragtag

Colonials and better equipped Redcoats takes place in view of his porch window.

After the battle, Martin's eldest son Gabriel is taken captive by the British as a spy, and his second-oldest son Thomas is cold-bloodedly executed by the Redcoats' steely officer, Colonel Tavington. The savage in Benjamin Martin finally cuts loose after years of dormancy.

Snatching up a tomahawk trophy from his old fighting days, some muskets, and conscripting two of his other boys as sharpshooters, Martin sets out to rescue Gabriel and get some payback. He makes good on both by massacring the column of Redcoats holding Gabriel captive with such blood lust that even his offspring are shocked.

Though initially against the war for independence ("This war will not be fought on the frontier or some distant battlefield, but among us—and the innocent will die with the rest of us," he observes presciently early on), he now enlists in the cause with a vengeance.

Appointed captain of a group of South Carolina militia, he launches a guerilla war against the British forces under Lord Cornwallis. Tactically his mission is to bog down Cornwallis's forces in the south so they can't go north to help destroy General Washington's Continental Army. Privately his mission is less patriotic: He just wants to spill as much British blood as he can, especially that of the hated Colonel Tavington.

But before the last fadeout, Martin comes to the realization that while revenge may be sweet, freedom is sweeter. He does settle his private score with Tavington, but willingly puts off doing so until the greater, public good of victory and independence has been achieved.

Many reviewers noted similarities between *The Patriot*'s Benjamin Martin (a composite of several real-life revolutionary war figures including Francis Marion, a.k.a. "The Swamp Fox") and *Braveheart*'s William Wallace. Some even suggested that *The Patriot* was little more than a rehash of *Braveheart* and that Gibson was just repeating himself.

It's true that Mel Gibson's performance in *The Patriot* offers us no tour-de-force surprises. For example, his emotional breakdown when Gabriel is killed later in the film doesn't astonish us with its acting power (which is still considerable) because we've already seen Gibson explode with this same kind of raw, human vulnerability in *Ransom*.

Similarly, Benjamin Martin's revoltingly savage blood lust, which he reveals occasionally in *The Patriot*, was a self-destructive failing that the doomed William Wallace exhibited pervasively. By the same token, Benjamin Martin is *not* William Wallace redux. There are important differences between the two characters. And these differences may indicate why Gibson the actor was more attracted to starring in *The Patriot* than Ridley Scott's *Gladiator* (2000), which was also offered to him, and is actually closer in theme and character to *Braveheart* than is *The Patriot*.

The Patriot can be viewed as an alternate history of the type of character personified by William Wallace if he'd survived instead of being executed.

For example, having done his bit for his fellow highlanders, he'd probably have thrown off his violent ways for the pacifist lifestyle of a farmer (his main goal, next to winning freedom), probably married and raised a family, and left achieving final victory against England to the likes of Scottish noble Robert the Bruce. But then the maelstrom of revolution would reach his door, and he'd likely be drawn back into the storm. At which point, one might wonder what would have next happened to Wallace.

In a sense, *The Patriot* tells us by giving Gibson the opportunity to explore a what-might-have-been scenario in the form of a different character, Benjamin Martin. And the result is an interesting twist on an important point about the kind of flawed hero Gibson often plays, and has made his own. This time, it is not the flawed Gibson character whose example fosters greater leadership in someone else; he is instead the beneficiary of that example.

In his publicity rounds for *The Patriot*, the now forty-five-year-old Mel Gibson has quipped that he feels it's time for young Aussie studs like Heath Ledger, who plays his son Gabriel in the film, to assume the mantel he has long held as an action-movie hero. As if to underscore Gibson's point, *The Patriot* gives to Ledger's Gabriel the function that Gibson's type of screen hero, especially in *Braveheart* and the *Mad Max* series, usually serves. Here, Ledger is the headstrong, rebellious, seemingly irresponsible, patriotic, and hell-bent-for-action figure who teaches the responsible, tentatively pro-independence, and revenge-obsessed Gibson the qualities of true leadership.

Initially the motives of Gibson's Benjamin Martin are solely personal. His prize is Tavington's head, and he adopts a bloodthirsty take-no-prisoners attitude in his single-minded pursuit.

Ledger's Gabriel wants Tavington dead too, but sees a higher purpose: defeating Cornwallis and paving the way for America's victory in the war for independence. "There's time for revenge—but not now," Gabriel counsels Benjamin repeatedly. "Stay the course."

Ironically, the father wisely comes to heed Gabriel's counsel just as the son briefly, and

Benjamin Martin (Mel Gibson), sister-in-law Charlotte Seton (Joely Richardson), and the remainder of the Martin family seek respite from the war at a haven for freed and escaped slaves.

tragically, forgets it.

To flush out Martin (whom the Redcoats have nicknamed "The Ghost") and his guerillas, the loathsome Tavington takes some villagers prisoner and executes them. Among the victims is Gabriel's bride Ann. Emotionally this finally proves too much for Gabriel; overwhelmed by grief and a craving for revenge, he spins wildly out of control, goes after Tavington himself, and is killed. He fails to get revenge or achieve his higher, nobler goal.

Though just as grief-stricken and vengeful over losing Gabriel to Tavington, Gibson's character is motivated by the loss to overcome (or at least suppress) his private demons and "stay the course," as his son had wished. He becomes the leader (and "Patriot" of the title) that his son's example paved the way for, the leader who is needed to hold off Cornwallis's forces and turn the tide of the war against the British.

WHAT WOMEN WANT

2000—PARAMOUNT PICTURES

"I know just as little now about what women want as I did when I started. And I came to the conclusion that that's by a very clever design, and it's intended that there are aspects of men and women that are meant to be a mystery."

—MEL GIBSON

CREDITS

Producers: Matt Williams, Susan Cartsonis, Gina Matthews, Bruce Davey; *Director:* Nancy Meyers; *Screenwriters:* Josh Goldsmith, Cathy Yuspa; *Cinematographer:* Dean Cundey; *Editors:* Stephen A. Rotter, Thomas J. Nordberg; *Composer:* Alan Silvestri; *Production designer:* John Hutman; Running time: 127 minutes.

CAST

Mel Gibson *(Nick Marshall);* Helen Hunt *(Darcy Maguire);* Marisa Tomei *(Lola);* Mark Feuerstein *(Morgan);* Lauren Holly *(Gigi);* Ashley Johnson *(Alex);* Delta Burke *(Eve);* Valerie Perrine *(Margo);* Alan Alda *(Dan Wanamaker).*

REVIEWS

"Usually cast in serious macho roles with the occasional soft streak, Gibson begins clearing a promising path for himself here as an unapologetic womanizer who's never willing to take no for an answer. Playing a man who's cocky, irrepressible, wild, crazy and always hot to trot, Gibson throws himself into even the most preposterous situations with such relish and abandon that the viewer, like most of the women, has little choice but to succumb to him, despite the prankish nature of what he's required to play."

—VARIETY, 12/11/00

"Gibson is so pumped for this change of pace, he's like a cork that's ready to pop. He clearly relishes mocking his macho image. Drunk on wine, he tests some female-oriented products that his agency may represent. Leg wax, padded bra, nail polish. Seeing him wiggle into control-top pantyhose is not a sight easily forgotten."

—USA TODAY, 12/14/00

"Mel Gibson looks a little old for this character and his comic timing is rather clunky, but he does have charm and good looks to spare. And what's more, he can dance"

—NEW YORK POST, 12/15/00

"Mel is swell, channeling the easy charm of a Cary Grant as he gamely waxes his legs and struggles with pantyhose in an effort to get a fix on the female

Nick (Mel Gibson) is transformed by his knowledge of what women want into the sensitive and caring male (with the looks of Mel Gibson) the film maintains is what every woman wants.

mystique. It is thanks mainly to that charismatic performance (and the opportunity to witness Mad Max have a close encounter with a pair of L'Eggs) that the otherwise unsatisfying production will nevertheless prove to be what audiences want on their holiday viewing menu."

—HOLLYWOOD REPORTER, 12/15/00

According to *What Women Want*, Mel Gibson's first foray into romantic comedy since the unfortunate *Bird on a Wire*, what women want is: someone like Mel

Gibson, who hangs on their every word. Also according to the film, this seems to be the *only* thing they want.

Given the fact that two of the film's three writers (one of them an uncredited Nancy Meyers) are women, that it was directed by a woman (Meyers again), and green-lighted by one of the most powerful (and rare) female executives (Paramount Motion Picture Studio Chairman Sherry Lansing) in Hollywood, this is a surprisingly antediluvian message for a film of any kind to make that is set in the postfeminist era of the new millennium. But then again, while everything on the surface of *What Women*

Creative whiz Helen Hunt lands the ad agency job coveted by chauvinist Mel Gibson because she knows What Women Want.

Want says NOW, its heart and mind, as well as its soundtrack, belong to yesterday.

Whereas *Bird on a Wire* sought to recall the classic screwball comedies of the 1930s and failed, *What Women Want* strives to throw us back to the classic chauvinist-male versus independent-woman square-offs between Spencer Tracy and Katharine Hepburn in films like *Woman of the Year* (1942). Mostly, it succeeds.

Mel plays Nick Marshall, a womanizing Chicago adman who loses the coveted post of creative director at his agency to a female rival (Helen Hunt); she gets the job over him, explains Mel's boss (Alan Alda), because the marketplace these days is female-driven and the agency needs a creative director who gets "into women's psyches, not their pants."

Nick's chauvinistic pride and professional self-esteem suffer a blow. In the belief that "there's too much estrogen in advertising these days," he sets out to "learn how to think like a broad."

In a now-famous set-piece, Mel's macho character dons makeup, paints his fingernails and toenails red, waxes his legs, and struggles into a body stocking to get a feel for what it takes to "look like a woman."

"They're insane! Why would anyone do that more than once?" he remarks, shortly before an accident with a hairdryer literally shocks him into hearing the private, personal thoughts of every woman he subsequently meets. As one of their thoughts is that he's not the gift to women he thinks he is, but an "asshole," comes as another shock to his system.

Unable to get the cacophony of female voices out of his head, he tries to re-create the bathroom accident in an effort to "turn me

Mel's macho character dons makeup, paints his fingernails and toenails with red polish, and waxes his legs to find out what it takes to "look like a woman." He concludes: "They're insane! Why would anyone do that more than once?"

back into me again," but the attempt backfires. A second-round jolt courtesy of a bolt of lightning makes his newfound talent stronger than ever.

A visit to a female shrink (played by an unbilled Bette Midler), whom he convinces of his "gift," results in a change of heart when she counsels: "Men are from Mars, women are from Venus. You speak Venusian. Why do you want to get rid of a wonderful gift like this?"

Suddenly, he realizes he can use his gift to his advantage. He can manipulate the usurper Hunt and upstage her right of out of the job she stole from him without her ever being the wiser.

Of course, you can see what happens next—in fact, you can see every single payoff to every single setup in this film's unfailingly pre-

Mel Gibson with director (and uncredited cowriter) Nancy Meyers on the set of What Women Want.

dictable plot coming well before it arrives.

In the course of perpetrating his under-handed scheme, Mel and Hunt fall for each other; he experiences a sense of shame when the scheme works and she gets ousted; he comes clean to her about what he's done, and how; loses his "gift;" but in the process has gotten in touch with his feminine side and transformed *Tootsie*-style into the genuinely sensitive and caring male (with the looks of Mel Gibson, of course) that the filmmakers insist is every woman's want.

Maybe they're right. *What Women Want* was one of the biggest hits of Mel Gibson's career, particularly with women.

Stretching the audience's support again in typical Gibson fashion, Mel's character is established for us at the outset, courtesy of a female narrator, as "a man's man, a leader of the pack that other men look up to and admire, but never gets what women want."

His self-absorbed "guy's guy" persona makes him a natural foil for a Tracy/Hepburn-style battle of the sexes with Hunt's character, who is established before we meet her as a "maneater" and a "bitch."

But neither character lives up to the negative billing.

Still smarting, perhaps, from the imbroglio with writer-director Brian Helgeland over how much of a bad guy to make his bad guy in *Payback*, Mel's Nick Marshall isn't a misogynist creep like the guys in *The Company of Men* (1997), nor intrinsically obnoxious like a Tim Allen (the actor for whom the role of Nick was originally intended). He's really a softy at heart—an imperfect husband (now divorced), an imperfect dad (to his estranged teenage

Believing "there's too much estrogen in advertising these days," Nick (Mel Gibson) sets out to "learn how to think like a broad."

daughter), and an imperfect lover (despite what he thinks)—who doesn't know any better about how to interact with women because he was born and raised in Las Vegas, where his mother was a showgirl; so he's simply accustomed to viewing females as "babes."

And Hunt's character meanwhile is really just a nice, sweet gal who is misunderstood by the male of the species, and deeply hurt by that misunderstanding.

As a result, all ends well without too bruising a donnybrook between them come the fadeout; she gets her job back, fires him (which he admits he deserves), and they go off together in a clinch feeling too marvelous for words.

What Women Want might have been funnier if it had been edgier. But it probably wouldn't have been as romantic if it had been edgier or

funnier. Though it runs long for a comedy (over two hours), it moves briskly. Despite some meandering subplots—involving Marisa Tomei (wasted as an aspiring actress Mel uses his gift to bed then let down sweetly), and a wallflower female employee whom he rescues from possible suicide—that add nothing but padding and sidetrack the main story, *What Women Want* is lively entertainment. It has a lot of heart, a great playlist of old love ballads sung by the likes of Sinatra, Sammy Davis Jr., and Peggy Lee, and it gives Mel mucho opportunities, macho and otherwise, to wow his fans.

The previously described makeup scene may be the most hyped of Mel's star turns here. But for my money the showstopper is his surprising solo dance routine, which he pulls off with the panache of a Bob Fosse.

229

MILLION DOLLAR HOTEL

2001—LIONS GATE FILMS

"It is lyrical and heart-rending on the one hand, but on the other, it is very bizarre and darkly comic."

—MEL GIBSON

CREDITS

Producers: Deepak Nayar, Bono, Nicholas Klein, Wim Wenders; *Director:* Wim Wenders; *Screenwriter:* Nicholas Klein, story by Bono and Nicholas Klein; *Cinematographer:* Phedon Papamichael; *Editor:* Tatiana S. Riegel; *Composers:* Bono, Brian Eno, U2; *Production designer:* Robbie Freed; Running time: 122 minutes.

CAST

Jeremy Davies *(Tom Tom);* Milla Jovovich *(Eloise);* Mel Gibson *(Skinner);* Peter Stormare *(Dixie);* Jimmy Smits *(Geronimo);* Gloria Stuart *(Jessica);* Donal Logue *(Best);* Bud Cort *(Shorty);* Amanda Plummer *(Vivien);* Harris Yulin *(Stanley Goldkiss);* Julian Sands *(Terence Scopey);* Tim Roth *(Izzy Goldkiss).*

REVIEWS

"There's a welcome level of irony present in Gibson's work; he tackles a nearly impossible character with charm and an edginess that give the film a much-needed center."

—VARIETY, 2/10/00

"[The Million Dollar Hotel] is likely to elicit a love-it-or-hate-it response from most viewers, and this explains why a movie with Mel Gibson, excellent in one of his most complex roles, has sat on the shelf for more than a year."

—LOS ANGELES TIMES, 2/2/01

"A major redeeming feature of the film—and its biggest surprise—is Gibson's enjoyably deadpan performance as the FBI agent who feels a connection with the hotel's residents because he grew up among 'Freaks' (he was born with a third arm sprouting from his back and now wears a neck brace). It's his best performance in years, and it's a shame the movie wasn't centered on his enjoyably nutty character."

—NEW YORK POST, 2/2/01

"The only escapee from this artfully distressed fruit basket is Gibson, who seems fully aware that he's caught in a stinker. Gibson affects the deep, 'I'm not fooling around here' voice of a straight-arrow G-man, and in every line reading you can hear him trying to put an ironic distance between himself and the ludicrousness of the proceedings. It's an actor's saving sanity, and it makes him look like the one

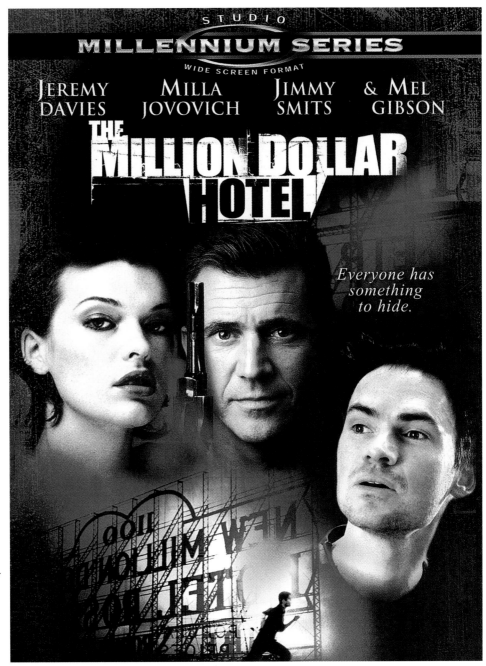

STUDIO
MILLENNIUM SERIES
WIDE SCREEN FORMAT

JEREMY
DAVIES

MILLA
JOVOVICH

JIMMY
SMITS

& MEL
GIBSON

THE MILLION DOLLAR HOTEL

*Everyone has
something
to hide.*

Despite the marquee value of Mel Gibson's name, The Million Dollar Hotel *wasn't picked up for U.S. distribution for almost a year. It went to video two months later.*

guy at the party who hasn't been dipping into the Quaaludes and laughing gas."

—SALON, 2/2/01

Something must have happened (or *not* happened) from script to screen because by the time the print was dry, Mel Gibson's feelings about *The Million Dollar Hotel* were no longer as positive as those that head this chapter. In fact, he had gone on record in

The Hollywood Reporter with the statement that the film was "as boring as a dog's ass."

I'm not sure I get the precise meaning of this critique (maybe it's an Australian colloquialism), but the gist is pretty clear. That this less-than-stellar endorsement came from Mel Gibson himself—who not only starred in the film but had a financial stake in it as well (his own company, Icon Productions, made it)—did not bode well.

Most U.S. distributors agreed. Despite the marquee value of Mel Gibson's name, the film—which premiered at the Berlin International Film Festival (where it was jeered) in February 2000—didn't get a U.S. release until the following year. (Though shot after *The Million Dollar Hotel,* both *The Patriot* and *What Women Want* were released in the U.S. before it, which is why I've placed it here in the chronology of Mel's films.)

On the strength of Mel Gibson's participation, *The Million Dollar Hotel* was eventually picked up by the independent distributor Lions Gate Films, which shoved it into theaters without ceremony, where it sank at the box office without a trace. The superstar has had his share of box-office underperformers in his career, but this was his first outright bomb. In one of the fastest turnarounds ever for a film with a major star, it went straight to home video a scant two months later.

So, how much of a mess is the film really? I'll put it this way. *The Million Dollar Hotel* has a lot in common with a car accident that you're not involved in. You can't help gawking as you pass by, but once it's gone, it's fast forgotten.

The movie's nut-job characters offer much to gawk at but leave no lasting impression—except for Mel Gibson's character, who is not only the least annoying but has the best lines. (Some of which are distinctly Mel-like and were probably improvised, as when his character puns, "I'm starvin'. I could eat a whore."]

He plays a maverick FBI agent named Skinner (a nod to *The X-Files,* maybe?) investigating the suspicious death of a billionaire's son who took a dive from the roof of an old hotel in downtown Los Angeles that is now the domain of mental patients and the homeless cast off by the city's welfare and health-care systems.

On the surface, the death looks to have been a suicide. But Skinner is convinced it was murder, and he has no shortage of suspects. Among them:

- The dead man's messianic Indian roommate Geronimo, well-played by Jimmy Smits.

- A John Lennon–wannabe, played amusingly by Peter Stormare.

- A retarded man on a skateboard, played convincingly by Jeremy Davies.

- A foul-mouthed grandma, played by Gloria Stuart in her second role aboard a sinking ship after years in retirement.

- A barefoot beauty with a Joan of Arc look about her, played by Milla Jovovich (who actually played Joan of Arc in Luc Besson's *The Messenger*).

- Too many more to mention.

Determined to wrap up the case quickly and get back to his demanding fiancee (who keeps pestering him with "where-the-hell-are-you" phone calls), Skinner fits in well with this group. He's henpecked on the personal front, but a Jack Webb–like tough guy (brush cut and all) on the job—"No matter how strange or despicable you act, I can do you one better because I work for the government," he barks at the hotel residents.

Ramrod straight and stiff-necked from a brace he wears from an old surgery that removed a third arm which grew from his back ("I could play the violin and wipe my ass at the same time"), Skinner was a freak in the circus before joining the FBI. As a result, he feels a growing kinship with these whackos, and comes to sympathize more with them than with the billionaire who lost his estranged son.

Eventually the mystery of whodunit is untangled. One could only wish that everything else about this confused mixture of science-fiction (the film is set in 2034) and film noir elements with fuzzy social commentary concocted for the screen by the lead singer of the band U2 was even as remotely straightforward.

Still, for fans and completists, *The Million Dollar Hotel* is a must-see because of Mel's winningly offbeat performance in a very different (even for him) kind of lead role played as a character part. And since most will have to catch this performance on video now because of the film's fast disappearance from theaters, they have a distinct advantage. They don't have to sit through the whole thing; they can search for Mel's scenes and fast forward through the rest with the remote control.

Awards—
AND THE WINNER IS . . . MEL GIBSON!

1998

- Blockbuster Entertainment Award for Best Actor in a Suspense Film—*Conspiracy Theory.*

1997

- People's Choice Award for Favorite Actor—*Ransom.*

- Blockbuster Entertainment Award for Best Actor in a Suspense Film—*Ransom.*

- Harvard Hasty Pudding Award for Actor of the Year.

1996

- Academy Award for Best Picture—*Braveheart.*

- Academy Award for Best Director—*Braveheart.*

- Golden Globe Award for Best Director—*Braveheart.*

- National Association of Theater Owners (NATO)

- ShoWest Award for Best Director—*Braveheart.*

- American Cinematheque Award for Best Director—*Braveheart.*

- British Academy of Film and Television Artists (BAFTA) Award for People's Choice

of Best Film of 1996—*Braveheart.*

- *Empire** Award for Best Director—*Braveheart.*

- Music Television (MTV) Movie Award for Best Action Sequence—the Battle of Stirling in *Braveheart.*

- People's Choice Award for Favorite Actor—*Braveheart*

- *E!* Entertainment Television's Golden Hanger Award for Best-Dressed Male Star, 1996.

1993

- Music Television (MTV) Movie Award for Best Action Duo—*Lethal Weapon 3.*

1991

- William Shakespeare Award—*Hamlet.*

1990

- People's Choice Award for Favorite Actor—*Lethal Weapon 2.*

1981

- Australian Film Institute Award for Best Actor—*Gallipoli.*

1979

- Australian Film Institute Award for Best Actor—*Tim.*

- Australian Film Institute Award for Best New Newcomer.

---

*Empire is a mass-market film and entertainment magazine published in the United Kingdom that is similar in style and content to the American magazine *Premiere.*

Bibliography

Periodicals

Abramowitz, Rachel. "Dressed to Kilt." *Premiere* 8, no. 9: 74–78.

_____. "Mad Mel." *Premiere* 7, no. 1: 46–52.

Anonymous. "Pat and Mel in '96?" *George*, June-July, 1996: 52.

Anonymous. "Gibson Gets Paid." *Billboard* 108, no. 11: 5.

Anson, Robert Sam. "Fly the Friendly Skies." *Premiere* 4, no. 1: 70–78.

Ascher-Walsh, Rebecca. "Ransom." *Entertainment Weekly* 352: 20–24, 27.

Cahill, Tim. "The Year of Living Carefully." *Premiere* 2, no. 4: 88–96.

Clarkson, Wensley. "Mel Gibson: Hollywood's Mischievous Maverick." *Cosmopolitan* 216, no. 4: 164–74.

Darrach, B. "Mad Max Plays Hamlet." *Life* 14, no. 2: 36–44.

Fuller, Graham. "Thistle Do Nicely." *Interview* 25, no. 5: 66–67.

Grobel, Lawrence. "Mel Gibson Interview." *Playboy* 42, no. 7: 51–63.

Gordinier, Jeff. "About Face." *Entertainment Weekly* 213: 7.

Hirschberg, L. "Mel Gibson." *Rolling Stone*, January 1989: 38–43.

Johnson, William. "Forever Young." *Film Comment* 30, no. 3: 76–80.

Jones, C. "My Six Kids Come First." *Redbook* 175, no. 4: 40–41.

Lahr, John. "Mel Gibson: Hollywood's Male Man." *Cosmopolitan* 209, no. 6: 160–65.

_____. "Road Worrier: Mel Gibson on Hamlet." *Harper's* 281, no. 1683: 32.

Laskas, Jeanne Marie. "The Sexiest Daddy Alive." *Redbook* 180, no. 1: 110–17.

Lewis, Kate Bohner. "Scottish Skinflint." *Forbes* 156, no. 7: 19–20.

Mansfield, Stephanie. "Mad Mac." *Gentleman's Quarterly* 65, no. 5: 140–46.

McCarty, John. "The Films of Peter Weir." *Video Times* 3, no. 5: 26–27.

McGuigan, C. "Melancholy Mel Goes to Elsinore." *Newsweek* 116, no. 27: 61.

Millea, Holly. "To Mel and Back." *Premiere* 10, no. 4: 86–90, 92, 94, 142–43.

Mills, Bart. "Mel Gibson: Still Growing Up." *Saturday Evening Post* 265, no. 6: 40–43.

Pelletier, Micheline. "Mel Gibson." *People Weekly* 39, no. 17: 86.

Ragan, David. "A Sheep in Wolf's Clothing." *Good Housekeeping* 216, no. 1: 34–37.

Ryan, Mo. "Hero's Reward." *Cinescape* 3, no. 2: 30–34.

Schaefer, Stephen. "Gluteus Madmaximus." *Entertainment Weekly* 276: 8.

Schruers, Fred, and Zahedi, Farooz. "How the West Was Fun." *Premiere* 7, no. 10: 46–53.

Sekoff, R. "Mel-o-drama." *Seventeen* 50, no. 1: 76–77.

Stivers, Cyndi. "Hamlet revisited." *Premiere* 4, no. 6: 50–56.

Thompson, Anne. "Mel in the Money." *Entertainment Weekly* 318: 14.

Watson, Albert. "The Maverick." *Vanity Fair* 428: 238.

Books

Brownlow, Kevin. *David Lean: A Biography*. St. Martin's Press: New York, 1996.

Koch, C. J. *The Year of Living Dangerously*. Penguin Books: New York, 1979.

McNeil, Alex. *Total Television*. Penguin Books: New

York, 1984.

Murray, Scott. *The New Australian Cinema.* Elm Tree Books: London, 1980.

Noble, Sandy. *The Unofficial Mel Gibson.* Parragon Book Service, Ltd.: Bristol, England, 1996.

Ozer, Jerome S., ed. *Film Review Annual.* James S. Ozer Publishers: Englewood, N.J., 1982-1994.

Perry, Roland. *Lethal Hero: The Mel Gibson Biography.* Oliver Books: Somerset, England, 1993.

Ragan, David. *Mel Gibson.* Dell Publishing Co.: New York, 1985.

Schickel, Richard. *Clint Eastwood.* Alfred A. Knopf: New York, 1996.

Silverman, Stephen M. *David Lean.* Harry N. Abrams, Inc.: New York, 1989.

Wicking, Christopher, and Tise Vahimagi. *The American Vein.* E. P. Dutton: New York, 1979.

About the Author

John McCarty is the supervising writer and codirector of the syndicated television series *The Fearmakers: Screen Masters of Terror and Suspense,* based on his 1994 St. Martin's Press book of the same name. The series was produced by the Dallas-based Group II Entertainment in conjunction with Otherstream Entertainment and is distributed by Planet Pictures. Mr. McCarty has also appeared on A&E's *Biography* series.

He was born in Albany, New York, in 1944. A movie fan since he was five, he began making his own films as a hobby in his early teens. After graduating high school in 1962, he attended Boston University, where he majored in communications (broadcasting and film). Following a stint in the Peace Corps, where he worked as an educational television volunteer in Bogotá, Colombia, he returned to the States and worked in broadcasting for a number of years, then became an advertising copywriter for the General Electric Company. He left that in 1983 to become a full-time author. His affection for the horror-film genre (and concern with what

was happening to it) led to his writing *Splatter Movies: Breaking the Last Taboo of the Screen* (St. Martin's Press, 1984). The book has become a worldwide cult classic and was followed by two companion volumes, *John McCarty's Official Splatter Movie Guide Vols. 1 and 2* (St. Martin's Press, 1989, 1992). His many other books about the world of motion pictures and motion-picture makers include *Hollywood Gangland* (St. Martin's Press, 1993); *Movie Psychos and Madmen: Film Psychopaths From Jekyll and Hyde to Hannibal Lecter* (Citadel Press, 1993); *Thrillers: Seven Decades of Classic Film Suspense* (Citadel Press, 1992); *The Modern Horror Film: 50 Contemporary Classics* (Citadel Press, 1990); *The Complete Films of John Huston* (Citadel Press, 1992); and *Alfred Hitchcock Presents: The Ten-Year Television Career of the Master of Suspense* (St. Martin's Press, 1985). He is also the author of the horror novel *Deadly Resurrection* (St. Martin's Press, 1990), which was recommended for a Bram Stoker Award as Best First Novel by the Horror Writers of America.